Praise for Wisdom in the Weeds

We all have those moments in our life we would like to forget. Or maybe even erase if we had a magic wand. Some of those experiences live in our thoughts, showing up at a random cadence. Others have almost vanished but for a particular interaction, sound, smell, or touch that brings it rushing back into our conscience. The recoil is real. Alyssa provides a beautiful reminder to embrace the mess and inconsequential moments of our journey as she provides tools to consider how God is shaping us through the pain in this broken world. I am grateful for Alyssa's willingness to share wisdom discovered along her path while teaching us to overcome the fear of being honest about our own weed-filled stories. *Wisdom in the Weeds* is a must-read for anyone looking for purpose and joy in their journey.

Kristin Burford, Pastor

Whether for the reader personally or awareness of the people around you, Alyssa brings attention to the depth and desperation of our need to have a voice. Do not miss the heart of the struggling friend who seems to have it all together. Do not overlook the value of a spoken word. Do not miss the moment to influence another's life.

Brigette Green, Asbury University

As she shares her story of 'letting go' of hiding behind performance-based acceptance and accumulating grievances along the way, we see how the true picture of ourselves as God's image-bearer can emerge. With humility and vulnerability, Alyssa shares her life learnings in a way that will help others untangle some of the knots in their own story.

Cheryl Green, Director of UpWords Ministries

Practical. Kind. Gracious. Alyssa embodies all of these in this helpful collection. We each need a friend to lead us when the weeds become too much. You'll find that friend in these pages.

Max and Denalyn Lucado, Pastors

Wisdom in the Weeds is an incredibly authentic, vulnerable, and self-reflective collection of essays journeying through the brokenness of life in light of the only One who can make us whole. Growing up, my mom always seemed to find lessons in moments where all I could see was hurt, heartbreak, and disappointment. The lessons she shares will provide companionship as you are invited into healing and the opportunity to rewrite your narrative. The words in each chapter are a friend blowing wind in your sails, pointing you back to the truth, and challenging you to press on.

Maddy Reiman, Alyssa's Daughter and Encourager

Wisdom in the Weeds

Wisdom in the Weeds

Life Lessons Learned Along the Way

* Alyssa De Los Santos

Paperback ISBN 979-8-9850875-4-3

ePub ISBN 979-8-9850875-5-0

Library of Congress Control Number 2023911775

Cover artwork and design by Riki Yarbrough

Book Design and Editing by Renee Johnsen

Printed in the United States of America

Dedication

For Renee—
Your constant encouragement changed the way I viewed my writing and myself. Without you, I would not have stepped fully into this process. Everyone needs a Renee in their lives. You are a gem beyond description, and I hope to love you well until my life expires.

For my parents–
Thank you for introducing me to Jesus, the source of wisdom. That firm foundation held when everything else was shaky. Thank you for pursuing healing in him and staying present in the story through the hard and holy moments of being a family.

Contents

Introduction

The most frequent thing people tell me after hearing me speak is that I put words to how they felt but did not know how to articulate. I let those words ruminate for years, and then I spent one year writing "Moment of Truth Monday" posts on my website, and even as I wrote each one, I knew the project would one day become a book. What you now hold in your hands is a collection of essays I wrote in several different seasons of life and stages of healing and growth.

The "Moment of Truth Monday" posts and subsequent essays are still every bit a part of my soul, and the authenticity invites others into a deeper conversation. Walking through a season of significant dismantling, my way through the dark was to write. Finding a lesson in the middle of the storm, kept my head above water and my spirit anchored amidst the crashing waves.

Writing my way through the personal, relational, and church trauma, I began peeling back the layers to reveal what was really causing injury to my soul. Throughout the process, even in the most trying of seasons, I found treasures of wisdom among the rubble. That is the gift of doing the hard work. Although it feels like it might take you out, there is enough grace to point you in the direction of healing and hope if you stick it out.

Trauma is a funny thing. It is an invisible obstacle, and because the wounds are unseen, it is easy to put off the work required to heal. You know it is there, but until you are strong enough to consider the contents of the baggage, you just carry it around. Once I began to face and unpack the weight of trauma I carried for years, an inarticulate shift in my spirit occurred. The journey toward healing required a lot of work, and I assume that is what makes avoiding it so appealing.

My husband spent several of his early years as a waiter. When overwhelmed with tables, he used the term "in the weeds," implying circumstances where there is more to do than time and energy available. When we are in the weeds in life, we might find a situation overly frustrating or discouraging. It is the tension between now and not yet, and we often lose sight of a way through the challenge. This is the space where we are inclined to quit because the journey does not seem worth the effort, but if we remember there is wisdom to gain in the weeds, we will pursue the story all the way to the end.

We all get tripped up on the difficulties of life; problems are as inevitable as weeds in a garden. Things will get hard and messy. Relationships take work. Weeds are unavoidable. We can lay down all the weed barriers we want, but we will never be able to eliminate all the challenges. We can only control what we take away from the experience.

If you have ever picked weeds, you know the posture required to get the job done. You have to bend low to the ground, be in proximity to the problem, and pull hard. Because it can sometimes be hard to discern a weed from a thriving plant, examination is necessary. This is also true when we are in a difficult or weedy season of life, and when we choose to endure the discomfort of a temporarily bent low posture, we will discover this is where we grow. Sadly, it is easy to miss growth opportunities because we prefer to do without hardship, but we have lived just enough life to know that we don't usually get to choose our seasons.

In the ordinary journey of our lives, the gift of hardship is that wisdom is a possible byproduct. If we are willing to stick it out, we might be surprised to discover that the lesson we learn was designed to carry us through the next hardship. Sitting through the storm often results in hope for the next leg of the uphill climb we are destined to face.

Hope is my desire for you as you encounter the words poured out in this collection of essays. Hope is the anchor of the soul. It kept me upright when the waves of life were crashing all around, and it continues to keep me standing firm as scary moments of life continue to unfold. For those of you who are in a desperate season, borrowed hope is still hope. Do not be afraid to lean on someone else's hope until you have the strength to cultivate your own. We heal in the context of community, so don't be afraid to reach out for help.

If you are an avid reader or writer, I hope you find a line of craft that tickles your ear and stirs your own creative genius. If you are confused or discouraged, I hope you find a place to rest and belong within the lines on each page. If you feel hopeless, I trust you will hold on to the wisdom revealed in the following life lessons excavated from the rubble of shattered dreams and hard seasons. If all else fails, play the long game and look for wisdom in the weeds.

Alyssa

Preface

My story is full of hard turns and missteps. While you will hear about some sensitive moments in the life of my family, I trust you will find the through line of hope, healing, and lessons of wisdom grown in soil watered by many tears. My early years were full of struggle, but we were all reaching for something better. My parents were finding their way out of their own painful narratives, and my sisters and I had front row seats. Even in the middle of the storm, they took us to church. They introduced us to Jesus. They loved us in the way they knew how, blow ups and breakdowns did not change that. The narrative has changed for our family, and I am deeply grateful for the opportunity to walk in redeemed relationships. We found wisdom in the weeds, but not without putting in intentional effort.

A sign that read "the struggle is part of the story" used to hang in my classroom. The words were intended to be a motivation for my students, but the truth is they were a daily reminder for me. It served as a silent pep talk every time doubt entered my mind and threatened my purpose and fortitude. I wanted a better story, but I wanted a pathway through daily wins and happy experiences, not through struggle.

Except I am certain we learn more in the valley than on the mountaintop, and I know the valley well.

I have chosen poorly and gotten lost along the way more times than I care to recall, yet I do not wish things were different. At the point of pain and hardship, I was inclined to bail out, but as I stare back at previous chapters of my story, I see the value of walking through the dark valleys. From childhood trauma and my parent's divorce to my own forgotten dreams and divorce, I have seen long nights framed with fears and tears. I have battled the desire to give up and believed my life was a disappointment, but I continued to put one foot in front of the other.

When we fail to pursue and unwrap the gift birthed in the hard seasons, we lose stamina for the journey. Life is full of struggles. We endure delayed flights, bank overdrafts, rejections, strained communication, illness, and loss in the ordinary routine of a life well-lived. In the middle of the struggle, life continues. We have choices we get to make in the valleys. We can focus on the losses, or we can search for the lesson and subsequent wisdom to guide us in the next chapter.

● ● ●

We have a dozen Live Oak trees in our backyard. While I love the shade they provide, I fight with the prolific Oak upshoots every spring and summer. In a burst of high-hope living, I often put on my gardening gloves and attempt to remove the landscape eyesores. Before I sound too heroic, I should tell you we routinely defer to trimming the upshoots. It is an easy, temporary answer to a long-term problem, and it beats the unbelievable effort required to uproot the things. The upshoots are well-rooted and strong. Here's the thing about those upshoots, they indicate life. Dead trees do not produce upshoots, living ones do.

If I have breath in my lungs, hard things will surface. Painful situations are inevitable. Just as the weeds fill my garden without invitation and reside in unlikely places like the tiniest cracks on my driveway, weeds of life will move in as fast as a summer storm. It seems that the struggles in life indicate life itself. Among the weeds are the flowers.

Wisdom exists among the weeds. I am not just saying that as a pie in the sky phrase; I believe it. Gems can be found among the rubble, but without intentionality, the treasure will remain unearthed. Maybe looking for wisdom in the weeds is the gift from all my struggling. Finding life lessons in the weeds was my natural bent and the way I developed resiliency. Instead of hiding the struggle, which I believe is our instinct, I learned to lean into the uninvited turns along the path.

Former teachers used to rib me about never missing an opportunity to find a lesson in ordinary moments. While taking third graders on a field trip to a Christmas tree farm, a fellow teacher asked me a question from the back of the bus. It took me a few minutes to discern the sarcasm in his words. "Where is your white board?" Seeing the confusion on my face, he asked me if I was going to miss moments to impart lessons during the bus ride. My tendency to excavate a lesson from every moment became a joke among my colleagues and family. I was not trying to do that; it came as naturally as my next breath because we learn how to adapt to our environment and grow out of the struggle.

● ● ●

I do not have a green thumb, as evidenced by the innumerable barren pots on my back porch, but I read a tip about harvesting flowers that stuck with me, and since we are talking about plants and gardening, I thought you might want to know. Flowers are best harvested in the morning, not in the heat of the day. In the same way, we are not always able to excavate the beauty of the struggle at the height of the fight, but wisdom can eventually be harvested in the soil of our stories. Wait it out; when the heat passes, harvest the lesson. Keep going. Look for the good among the gross. It is there, but you will have to intentionally hunt for it.

As you encounter the essays in the pages that follow, I hope you are encouraged to find the wisdom born from your everyday struggles. Like the Oak upshoots in my backyard, if not dealt with, they will take over the soil and choke out the plants in proximity. They steal nutrients needed to nurture life and growth. Put in the time to do the work to deal with the hard seasons punctuated by weeds. You may need to seek professional help; we often need an outside voice to direct us on the inside job of healing.

Friend, please refrain from letting life's struggles keep you from living wholeheartedly. Weeds are inevitable; they point to fertile soil. Celebrate the evidence of life, not the inconvenience of the weed. Look for wisdom in the weeds.

SECTION ONE

Uprooting Fear

Chapter One

Let Courage be Greater than Fear

* Maybe my words were sent out when
  they needed to be taken in.

Courage is contagious. When a brave man takes
a stand, the spines of others are often stiffened.
—*Billy Graham*

I WAS IN MY FORTIES BEFORE I UNDERSTOOD the tight grip fear had on me. That is a whole lot of life and decisions laced in fear without even recognizing it. It wasn't until I attended a conference on childhood trauma and resilience that I even considered the full impact of my childhood. I knew my story had some sharp turns, but I assumed everyone had lived a fairly similar life.

It is easy to spot fear in someone else. As a mom, I routinely coached all three of my children out of fearfulness. My oldest feared not making the grades to get into college. His meltdown sophomore year while studying for a test told the whole story. He was sure a poor test grade would grossly impact his college, career, marriage, and housing options. He felt the ripple of fear flood his future.

My daughter battled the fear of not being good enough in her sport. She left no room for error in her practice that spilled into her personal life. Although she would be gracious toward others about their mistakes, I had to peel her off the ground after losses she interpreted as indictments on her identity. Fear bullied her toward false beliefs and a sense of hopelessness.

Our youngest had an extra measure of timidity that was rooted in fear. I will never forget a time in preschool when things came to a head. We had practiced his one line for the Thanksgiving performance, and while he was painfully shy, I just knew he could handle the moment. When it was his turn to deliver his line, he beelined off the stage and straight for his teacher's lap, not the microphone. I was mortified because it felt like my loss. A well-meaning parent turned to me with the encouragement that maybe one day he would be "normal."

Being present in a space where fear threatened was both a privilege and crazy difficult. One of my best parenting statements was to remind my littles to let their courage be greater than their fear. That encouragement was a recognition of the presence of fear and the confident belief that they had the strength to rise above. Maybe my words were sent out when they needed to be taken in. Do you find it intriguing that much of the advice we give to others we fail to implement ourselves?

For various reasons, I held on to the limiting belief that I had nothing to offer—no gifts or talents, no wisdom, no "good" thing. From this limiting belief, I made or did not make decisions. It was where I counted myself out before I even considered the circumstances. While I did not consciously agree with the limiting belief, it was as instinctive as ducking my head when entering a parking garage.

My tendency toward timidity subtly compromised my courage. It was not bigger than my fear, but you cannot address what you don't recognize. As it turns out, it would take me 40+ years to see how scared I had been my entire life. Scared that there wasn't a place for me to belong. Scared that I was always going to be behind. Scared that I was always going to have to work my butt off to keep up with others. Scared to step into the calling of my life. Being scared kept me small for much of my life.

While I was busy coaching my children out of the prison of their fears, I was missing my own paralysis. When we cower to fear, we don't just neglect moments to exercise courage; we sabotage opportunities. Fear makes us shortsighted. It compromises wisdom. Little things become deal breakers, and big things paralyze us.

● ● ●

My friend runs a ministry for the homeless community in our city. He talks about it with such passion that you cannot help but want to get involved. Unless you have layers of preconceived ideas about people experiencing homelessness. Unless you are afraid. Unless fear says to leave that job to someone else. For three years, I listened to his stories with some of the least of these. I wanted to go, but I was afraid of the unknown. I had not stepped foot into the arena of homelessness—except for the occasional fear-inducing encounters I had experienced downtown. I feared for my safety. I feared not being helpful. I feared my fear of it all.

Swallowing the pill I had routinely prescribed for my children, I resolved to let my courage be greater than my fear. I signed up to serve. Because fear subsides with familiarity, I recruited my husband and son to join me. It was painfully hot that June evening, but as sweat dripped off me, so did my fear. Before I knew it, hours had passed. As I served outside my comfort zone, the result was incalculable. My fear was arrested by my courage.

We served a meal, distributed clothing and snacks, and cut hair. Well, I didn't cut hair, and we can all be thankful for that, but trained barbers offered haircuts. It just so happens that the son of one of my friends stepped in that evening to help. I walked over to observe him and stumbled into a conversation that will remain with me for as long as my mind will house it.

When I asked the young man in the chair what he thought about his haircut, he told me about the last time he had a haircut, and I felt the fear rise. While serving time in jail, he went to see the barber before a court appearance. He spoke of another prisoner knocking out the barber in the middle of his cut. He laughed about the half-cut he wore in the courtroom. He told me of his journey with drugs and fights, losing his wife and three children, and wanting to find his way back to his beloved career. He had been a great chef in a local restaurant. I listened to every word because I was there as a fellow human who understood the power of loss and the fear that leaves when we experience authentic connection.

After several minutes of sharing, he circled back to my original question. My new houseless friend said the young barber cutting his hair was fantastic. He turned to him and said that if he approached life with the same confidence he had with the clippers in his hand, he would do well in life. I tried to hide the tears pooling in my eyes. Here was this man I would have feared two hours prior, speaking courage into another young man's life. He was being served and serving. In that moment, I realized that courage sometimes means showing up afraid and being willing to loosen the hold of preconceived labels.

Though I started from a place of fear, I left with a new understanding of the wisdom I had often overlooked in my parental coaching. Letting your courage be greater than your fear is an excellent exercise in moving out of a fixed mindset. Still, I had not understood the broader lesson from the conversation over a haircut in the sweltering summer heat. Courage can be feeling afraid and showing up anyway. You don't have to manufacture courage before doing something that elicits fear. Stepping into a situation framed in fear might be the decision that illuminates the courage you did not know you had.

Don't wait for the courage to do something you feel prompted to do. If you wait for courage, you might find that you will drown in fear and regret. The what-ifs of life can add unnecessary pain to an already difficult life. Recalling his regrets, the man sitting in the barber's chair told me how he wished he had made better choices. I looked him square in the eyes and said, "You don't have to look back in regret, you can live differently from today forward. Step courageously into one decision at a time. The rest of your life is in front of you, and I believe in you."

As I spoke those words of hope and belief into his life, I realized they were just as much for me. Fear has long kept me looking backward in regret, but courage compels me to look ahead and capture the moments to show up afraid. Yes, courage can be greater than our fear. I just forgot to tell my children and myself the rest of the story. Courage can also be the result of doing something outside your comfort zone. In deciding to move forward in trepidation, courage can come. It is often cultivated in the same soil as the fear.

As clumps of hair fell to the ground, I sensed the grip of fear loosening between us and around me. Every time I recognize the invitation of fear, I have a choice. I can let my fear be greater than my courage, or I can walk in courage even though I feel afraid. Fear has never been the problem. We all feel afraid. Making decisions from a place of fear stifles courage, and that is really the lesson I was trying to learn and teach my children. If I could add anything to the lesson, it would be this. Courage and fear can coexist.

Reflection: Has a limiting belief held you back? What role has fear played in your life? Is there something you are currently facing that sparks fear? Can you show up afraid? What might that look like?

Going Deeper: Read John 14:27. What does this passage say about fear? The verse says do not be afraid—not do not feel afraid. How does that change your view of fear? How does it reframe your idea of the possibility of fear and courage coexisting?

Chapter Two

Somewhere Between Fear and Freedom

* Fear functions like funhouse mirrors—
completely distorting the reflected
image.

Peace I leave with you; my peace I give you. I do not give to you as the world gives. Do not let your hearts be troubled and do not be afraid.
–Jesus

I AM A QUITTER. While I am not proud of this, it has been true of me more times than I care to admit. When tasks appear to be outside my skillset or comfort level, I defer to shrinking back and measuring all the reasons why I should abort the mission.

In seventh grade, I walked off the volleyball court during a game. My coach put me in a position I did NOT want to play. My complicated middle school emotions and inarticulate personal trauma told me I was not good enough. Armed with a lot of hurt and a skewed perspective, I changed out of my uniform, handed it to the coach, and rode the bus home as a quitter.

When relationships hit rough waters, my first tendency is to turn and run in the opposite direction. What precedes the instinct to run is an intense fear that I am not cut out for whatever is in front of me (no matter what that is).

Fear always drives my desire to quit. I have heard people say that fear stands for False Evidence Appearing Real. Fear functions like funhouse mirrors—completely distorting the reflected image. The trouble is, I buy into it with little persuasion or investigation into the validity of the distorted reflection. When I defer to fear, I develop immediate paralysis. Everything feels too overwhelming and way out of reach, so I give up. I freeze. I stop doing all I know to be good, true, and worthy.

Fear has a funny way of showing up. It may not show up in the form of quitting for you. You might be inclined to overeat, cry, binge-watch your favorite show, exercise, or overindulge in your favorite store's big sale. No matter how it shows up, we can indulge it or identify it for what it is and reject its power. Fear does not automatically have permission to bully us around. We do not have to listen to the tape repeatedly telling us we do not have what it takes to be successful. We can choose to cultivate fear or squelch it.

● ● ●

Being hyper-focused on short-term solutions is closely related to putting out small fires. We become distracted and consumed with what is right before us, and big-picture details fade. Fear and scarcity drive us to make decisions contrary to a well-measured response. The mix of the two can alter our outlook and motivate extreme choices.

While listening to an NPR podcast about the scarcity mindset, the host shared a simple and profound idea that resonated. When we do not have enough of something, which is a basic definition of scarcity, we lose focus. Think of it like putting out small fires instead of tending to the larger problem. We can find ourselves so hyper-focused on a quick solution that we fail to see the larger picture. Our motivations get blurred and our actions quickly follow.[1]

Not having enough of something is what happened to me on the seventh-grade volleyball court and with toilet paper during the COVID-19 pandemic. We traded the ultimate for the immediate. Fear drove us to scarcity because we were afraid there wouldn't be enough to go around. When we perceive a threat, we have an instinctual response. We do not all respond the same, but our parasympathetic nervous systems heighten, and we respond from that space. Sometimes we flee. Sometimes we freeze. Sometimes we hide. Sometimes we hoard.

I am no stranger to hoarding. Chick-fil-a sauce is my Achilles' heel. To be dignified, I order fries as a conduit for the sauce, but I am not above using my finger to finish the packet when the fries are gone. Some of you cannot understand this madness, but others know exactly what I mean. If, by some strange miracle, there is an extra sauce left after a meal, I gladly shove that treasure in my purse for future indulgence, forgetting that I can go back and enjoy it again. Because I defer to fear that there won't be enough, I make irrational decisions to put a flimsy packet in my purse, which is supposed to absolve my scarcity mindset.

While standing in a checkout line the other day, I was reminded of the price of hoarding tendencies. I reached into my purse, fished for my wallet, and paid my bill. As I put my wallet back in my bag, my hand skidded through something that appeared to be a mix of oil and wax. It was gooey, sticky, and gross. A fusion of panic and horror washed over me. My kids were equally humored and disgusted by the large glob on my small wallet. My headspace flooded with all the questions. What was the mystery substance? Where did it come from? Was there more yet to be discovered? Should I throw my purse away and start over?

Back at the car, I moved through the contents of my purse like a crime scene investigator. I pulled out my work badge; a mound of the same oil and wax concoction covered its surface. Leery, I carefully removed my coin purse, and it was covered with the same substance. In a flash, I knew exactly what had happened.

Chick-fil-A sauce.

A packet of sauce must have opened, spilled, and spewed all over the contents of my purse. I dug through all the unmentionables and years of rogue receipts and saw it. That extra packet I had eagerly saved had seen too many miles, and I had long forgotten it was even along for the ride.

I wish my hoarding tendency was limited to restaurant sauce, but it is not. My default is to hold tightly to what I have instead of sharing it freely. Fear has driven my decision to cling to what I have; it has shown up in subtle and overt ways.

- I have withheld encouragement from a loved one who desperately needed it.
- I have hidden the truth from a friend who wanted an honest response.
- I have been stingy with love because I was afraid to be vulnerable.
- I rehearse affirming lines for my family that never move from my head to my mouth.
- I shrink back when I need to step up.

Maybe this doesn't feel like hoarding to you; it wasn't until I understood scarcity that I saw my decisions for what they were. I was afraid of letting go of the little I had. My life experiences taught me to trust few and take care of myself because there was no way of knowing when the next provision would come.

My friend adopted a beautiful daughter a few years ago. She tells a story about finding food hidden in her daughter's bed and elsewhere around the house. Although initially perplexed, she realized the trauma of not knowing if and when the next meal would come had been seared on her daughter's conscience. Scarcity shows up in our behaviors and decisions.

Hoarding can be socially acceptable things. For instance, I love denim. If one pair of jeans is good, then ten pairs are obviously better. I own denim shirts in a variety of colors. If a girl could marry denim, this one already did. Are you tracking with me?

I used to think this obsession was limited to denim. I had convinced myself that

1. it was not actually a problem and
2. it was a useful hobby.

Other people like to run and sew, and I like denim—totally the same.

Pause.

Justifying behaviors is not a new practice. From the beginning of time, people have been justifying behaviors for the sake of their comfort and taking extreme measures to protect them.

Obsessions indicate extremes. Extremes are not always harmful but usually elevate focused attention from a healthy place to an excessive one. When I obsess about something, I lose focus, and I forget to see anyone or anything except the object of my desire. The problem is I long to be a person who contributes to the good of those around her. I want to love the marginalized, welcome the overlooked, and see the lonely. It is hard to achieve others-focused responses when my mind is set on my own desires. Vision turned inward disrupts outward focus.

Most of the time, my hoarding and extreme behaviors are well-rooted trauma responses. I lose sight of the priority of being connected, encouraging, and kind because I focus on the smoke screen of fear and scarcity. The worn path suggests duck and cover instead of stepping up and speaking out. What rises from the things I unconsciously withhold from others might look like jealousy, but it is not.

The opposite of a scarcity mindset, according to Brené Brown, is enough.[2] Instead of worrying about what you lack, you make mental notes of what you have. Noticing and choosing to be thankful is a perspective shift that moves us from clutching and withholding to engaging. When we are attuned to the reality that we have enough, we will be more inclined to give away than hoard. We will eventually begin to veer away from extremes and lean into moderation.

In an enough mindset, we...

- give away encouragement instead of keeping it to ourselves
- share our surplus resources with those in need
- celebrate the victories of others without feeling threatened
- tell others who we see them becoming
- leave room for ourselves and others to assume a new narrative

I am surrendering my habit of putting that extra Chick-fil-A sauce in my purse. If I stay in the moment, I avoid the fear of not having enough when the next time rolls around. From this exhale of fear and inhale of hope, I will scatter encouragement and kindness. I will forgive and seek forgiveness. I will share without fear.

The tendency to hoard is a survival mechanism, but it does not have to be mine. Will you take this step with me? Will you be gracious with encouragement? Will you share with someone in need?

Fear drives scarcity that impacts our focus and compels us toward hoarding. We can choose to get off that hamster wheel! There is a verse in the bible I have lived by and wielded no less than a million times in parenting, and my daughter has said she thinks it is etched on her femur bone!

All things are permissible, but
not all things are beneficial.[3]

Think about that. We have the freedom to do as we please—be it buy too many pairs of jeans, quit the team, drink too many cocktails, deceive a partner, exercise for hours on end, overspend, or commandeer extra condiments.

The second part of the verse is what I ask myself often. Is this beneficial? Sometimes it is, so it is good to follow that up with another reflective question. Who benefits from this, or what is the specific benefit to my family, friends, community, etc.?

A love for denim is not the real problem. Justifying extreme behavior is the issue. Where is the extreme behavior pointing?

Do you tend to justify behaviors or decisions? It may be time to explore how much control we have given over to fear and scarcity. What would happen if we stopped pardoning extreme behaviors as individuals, families, and communities? What might happen if we made personal decisions to quit quitting and stick things out through the messy middle?

We were uniquely created to contribute to our respective communities. It is high time we stand against fear, remember we have enough, and rein in extreme behaviors. The result is the freedom to show up and contribute what we have.

Somewhere on the other side of fear, scarcity, and extreme behavior is a spacious place of peace where we strike a balance between what is permissible and beneficial, and there we find wisdom in the weeds.

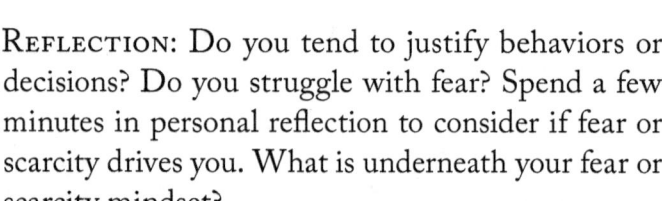

REFLECTION: Do you tend to justify behaviors or decisions? Do you struggle with fear? Spend a few minutes in personal reflection to consider if fear or scarcity drives you. What is underneath your fear or scarcity mindset?

Assuming the opposite of scarcity is enough, list all the things that can fall into your enough category. Consider keeping a journal of the gifts you experience in a week, month, and year. When you feel discouraged, read your list to remember your wins and shift your perspective.

GOING DEEPER: Read Philippians 4:1-8. What seems to be the antidote for fear? Close your time giving thanks for the gift of peace and provision in your life.

Chapter Three

Moving Through Fear

* When I give fear too much attention, I
  miss the opportunities in front of me.

*We can easily forgive a child who is afraid of
the dark; the real tragedy of life is when men are
afraid of the light.*
–Plato

IT WAS A MOVE I HAD TO MAKE after being
displaced from my teaching assignment. My unraveling
marriage and impending divorce deemed it necessary
for me to return to work, and it made no difference
that it was the day before school resumed. I was
the last hire on campus that year, and if you know
anything about schools, you know the last hire is the
first to be displaced. It was not personal; it was just
the nature of things.

While navigating the transition, I had the added
stress of contemplating the impact another adjustment
would have on my children. If you have not lived as
a single parent, you cannot grasp the immense pressure you feel to successfully fit one million moving

parts together. Every decision has a felt ripple effect; returning to work was not insulated from that.

Sitting in one of my interviews, I had a strong sense it was the school where I was being called. I have always viewed my profession as a calling. The bonus was that it would be a good fit for my children. Only one thing gave me pause, and it was a giant in my mind. The school was a Title I school. If you are unfamiliar, when 40% or more of a school's student population is enrolled in the free or reduced lunch program, the school qualifies for additional federal funding. I had a lot of teaching experience but zero at a Title I school.

I was afraid.

Fear does not usually make sense, and it is often anchored to a lack of experience.

I was afraid I would not know how to interact with the students; I was scared I would not know the best way to handle academic challenges.

In an act of tentative courage, I voiced my trepidation to my potential bosses. To my surprise, they did not meet my hesitation with shame. They responded with compassion. They attempted to assuage my fears. Ultimately, they poked holes in the fear without poking holes in me.

I knew I was called to the school for that season. I remember falling in love with my students on day one. Even though I was scared, I showed up anyway. The depth and reverberation of doing something afraid would become an Ebenezer moment for me—a time I knew God had intervened on my behalf.

One day, I was standing at the overhead projector (old school technology) when tears suddenly filled my eyes. Nothing was wrong; the students were doing what I had requested, but in a moment of absolute clarity, I realized my initial fear was unwarranted. It had always been so. It was a holy moment, one that will remain etched in my soul. Glancing from student to student, with the love of a mother, I was overwhelmed by one overriding thought. Kids are kids—period. My eyes bounced from student to student with an inarticulate joy as I absorbed the moment.

My students hailed from a variety of experiences and socioeconomic backgrounds. They were not comparing notes about either, though. They showed no signs of fear that I would somehow treat them poorly because I had not taught at a Title I school. It is unlikely that most of them even knew those words were attached to our school. They trusted me.

I knew; I was the one who was afraid.

While I do not know where that fear was born, discovering it, acknowledging it, and stepping through it was necessary to extinguish it. Fear can stymie faith and fan doubt into flame.

No matter how you frame life's experiences, it is important to assess your fears. Measure the validity of the fear, find a trusted friend who will hold space for you as you work through it, and sit in the tension of it all. Don't worry about your fear making sense to everyone in your life—or anyone at all. When we defer to stuffing our fears, they shape us in ways that no longer feel authentic to who we were created to be. Untempered fear bullies us into silence and prevents us from pursuing anything that would illuminate the powerlessness of what is causing our fear.

● ● ●

When my children were small, their nighttime fears often called me back to their rooms. Maybe they heard a noise or thought something was in the closet, and they did not care if I thought their fear was legitimate. Though often inconvenient, I did not offer a lecture on the absurdity of their claim or shame the feeling gripping them. I opened the closet, turned on a light, looked under the bed, held them tightly, and did all I could to quiet their fears.

They felt afraid, but they didn't have to be afraid.

Did you know there is a difference? Hundreds of times throughout scripture, we read the encouragement to be unafraid. Feeling afraid is a response to a situation, but being afraid is the decision to act from a place of fear. God comes into the times I feel afraid and comforts me, so I no longer have to be afraid.

45

That is what love does.
Love steps into scary situations.
Love comforts when fear threatens.
Love stays the course.
Love makes room for others. Period.

The gentleness of the Good Shepherd reminds me that I can act from a place of confidence instead of fear. That is the exact sense that washed over me in the classroom that day. My decision to move through my feeling of fear, not around it, taught me a lesson I have not soon forgotten. Poverty is a lack of financial resources; being poor in spirit is a posture of dependence.

While I am growing in my understanding of feeling afraid versus being afraid, I am still working to uproot the primary cause of my fear. It is one thing to be able to call a thing a thing, but it is altogether different to do the necessary work to experience lasting change. Let me illustrate this with my own life.

For much of my adult life, I have felt the call of leadership. Responding to the call has manifested in speaking at retreats and local women's events and organizing women's ministry events. The speaking opportunities have always been my favorite, but they have come in fits and spurts.

Much of the last ten years have been marked by a strong sense of striving. I have been genuinely afraid of what I might miss if I took a break. FOMO, fear of missing out, has not guided my journey well, yet I have not failed to invite it into nearly every season. Fear of missing an opportunity or being overlooked has kept me busy, burned out, and bitter. It has grossly impacted the way I negotiate the call on my life. I heard myself say the following words while sharing with a friend.

"I don't need to be a writer. I don't need to be a speaker. I can just be a high school teacher, call it done, and be fulfilled, but I wonder if my lack of contentment is a result of settling for a lesser thing. I have a history of God calling me to something that I reduce to manageable parts that do not require supernatural influence. When I make things manageable, I can execute the task, but I lack satisfaction because I have not completely submitted to the broader dream. Reducing a call to what my mind can understand alters the risk and impacts the result."

The words I spoke aloud reverberated in my soul and haunted my mind, and I knew I needed to consider them in a new way. What was my *why* anchored to? Why did I endeavor to write a weekly post when I sensed a clear prompting to start a podcast? When prompted to take those weekly posts and create a book, why did I reduce that to a short devotional? Why was my instinct to stop before I even started?

You know the answer, right? You may be acutely familiar with the reason. Fear. What if I failed? What if I didn't know what to do? What if the task out-measured my ability and know-how? I have a long history of relying too much on my own understanding because trusting others is risky, and my vulnerability has not been protected or respected by people I expected to be faithful and true.

Can you hear the echo of spiritual poverty? The unknown in my classroom experience hardly differs from the unknowns in my calling and life. Faith and fear pull on the same strings of courage, and they beckon me to decide which one will win. When fear wins, I walk in self-reliance and self-preservation. I fatigue easily. Discouragement comes quickly when I cannot see a way out. When faith wins, I step forward. Sometimes my knees are wobbly, and my heart beats out of my chest, but, nevertheless, I walk.

● ● ●

My youngest son was born with an extreme bent toward shyness. He spent most of his first week in kindergarten sitting under the table, not at it. Watching it was painful, so I never could imagine how it pulled on his tiny heart and mind. When we would do anything for the first or fiftieth time, I would turn to him and say the following words, "Let your faith be bigger than your fear."

I am taking a page from my own book. My faith must be bigger than my fear. Fear is a lousy travel companion, and it most definitely gives a bum steer on life's journey. When I give fear too much attention, I miss the opportunities in front of me. I don't want to be known for shrinking back and living in regret, so today I am consciously deciding to move through fear with the strength of faith.

Do you have a history of shrinking back or being bossed around by fear? Stop tiptoeing around it; call a thing a thing, punch fear in the face, and move through it. Yes, it may be difficult, and quitting may seem like the better prospect, but the new depth of freedom is worth the investment.

We can feel afraid, but may we also have enough courage to avoid making decisions in fear. Moving through fear offers a new perspective, and it lifts our gaze from circumstances to possibilities. The work isn't easy, but looking for wisdom in the weeds will always be worth the process.

REFLECTION: If we don't name our fears, they will name us. What are the fears you entertain in the quiet places of your mind? Once you acknowledge your fears, they will lose the power of their previous persuasion.

GOING DEEPER: Read Psalm 23. What comfort do you find in these words? What is the antidote to your fear?

Chapter Four

Perfectionism: The Response of an Attention-Starved Soul

* We get to choose what gets our attention, so we have more control than we may understand.

At its root, perfectionism isn't really about a deep love of being meticulous. It's about fear. Fear of making a mistake. Fear of disappointing others. Fear of failure. Fear of success.
–Michael Law

PERFECTIONISM IS AS EASY as swimming upstream in level five rapids with a millstone tied around your neck. Nothing is predictable or easy for the perfectionist, and life's trajectory under such weight runs counter to the intended outcome. Ask me how I know.

I heard a pastor share the following statement. "Certainty is knowing how. Confidence is knowing who."⁴ The phrase stirred something deep in the fibers of my being, so I wrote it down and have returned to it time and time again. The words felt like home, but I struggled to fully comprehend the connection to certainty and a life burdened by the need for things to appear perfect.

For much of my life, I prided myself on knowing how. This bent served me well in my profession as an educator. Numbers and scores matter, and my overcommitment to work made what was happening in my classroom stand out. When something serves you well in the immediate, it is hard to see the need for a future adjustment. The work behind my striving garnered praise, and I was a girl starved for attention, so my tendency to run hard persisted.

There must be numerous reasons one turns toward perfectionism. I will not dare to diagnose why; I will defer to trained professionals to explain the ins and outs of where we develop tendencies toward perfectionism, but I will pull back the curtain to show you how it came to be part of my life. Brace yourself because the following could trigger your trauma.

An intense fear marked my early childhood years. Our four walls housed fighting that often turned into episodes of violence. While I did not know that was what the outside world would call it, I knew it robbed me of a sense of security. My nervous system was perpetually heightened because there was no way to forecast the next storm. I spent a lot of time alone and hiding, and the seed of feeling unseen was planted and then germinated in the silence of my mind.

School became my escape. It was a necessary break from the inconsistencies of home, and my teachers seemed to notice me. If I worked hard and did well, I would get positive attention from the staff. The benefit of perfectionism and striving filled my tattered heart, and I had no clue my feet were set on a pathway toward destruction. Looking back now, I wonder what the teachers saw when they looked at me. Could they see the depth of despair I carried into the classroom? Did they know I was attention starved? Was I the student they lamented about around their dinner table? Did they notice the way I drank up their praise?

The fighting at home intensified and it was not long before my parents announced their intention to divorce. My sisters and I had to find a new sense of normal. You might not know this, but when you live in dysfunction, it is your "normal" even when it is anything but. We rarely talked with our parents about the heavy weight we carried, which made space to create another chapter in the false narrative I was writing. If I had worked harder to be good, maybe things would be different in my relationship with my parents and their relationship with each other. This was never something I articulated, but the thought was always there.

●　●　●

If you live with a perfectionist, you know how hard expectations land on others. But I am here to tell you that no matter how hard it is to live with a perfectionist, you have no idea how hard it is for perfectionists to live with themselves. I mean that.

The outward pressure on others is easier than the standard perfectionists hold themselves to. While I cannot fully explain that, I know those who tend toward perfectionism just said *amen*. The inner critic of a perfectionist delivers devastating blows that continue the striving to be better and do better. Imagine the negative tape that reminds you of all the ways you failed in life. That is a tiny glimpse of the inner world of a perfectionist.

The circumstances of my childhood, the fighting, divorce, and subsequent years of longing to be seen and nurtured led me to believe that I was not valued, so I developed a habit of working hard to prove my value. What followed was a long list of decisions someone confident in their worthiness would not make. I will spare you the specific details, many of which I am anything but proud of, but the vices, the relationships, and the lack of self-care were evidence my life was not on a healthy trajectory.

In the soil of unworthiness, perfectionism grew silently but also prolifically. To be clear, this was not because I wanted to be perfect, it was because I wanted to know I was valuable, and I truly believed the only way to do that was to show how valuable I could be. My view of myself was marred by lies embedded in the fabric of my life. I believed I was bad, and the only way out was to prove otherwise. This landed me in a place of burnout because I was always striving and rarely resting. Rest is not the standard dialect for a perfectionist.

What I have shared may give you insight about someone in your life. Maybe this is the insight you needed for yourself. Either way, let this truth be something that grows your compassion for those who wrestle with type A behaviors. Most perfectionists are hungry to hear someone near them say they are doing a good job. Rewrite the narrative you may have developed about perfectionists. Encourage rest. Celebrate their work but invite your favorite perfectionist to exhale and sit in moments where they are not expected to do anything except receive.

In her book, *The Gifts of Imperfection: Let Go of Who You Think You're Supposed to Be and Embrace Who You Are*, Brené Brown emphasizes the difference between healthy striving and perfectionism.[5] She explains that striving can be healthy when it is focused on improving oneself, but perfectionism becomes unhealthy when it is focused on what other people think. Perfectionism leads to burnout, mental health issues, and fatigue because perfectionism always points us to what we can do, prove, or explain to win the approval of others. There is no rest for the perfectionist because there is always more to do, and the standards of others may be unattainable.

While I know it is not true for everyone, my perfectionistic tendencies were rooted in an unworthy posture. I cared too much about what other people thought and too little about improving myself for the sake of myself. When you lack worthiness, you lean toward working to attain value. You can use this as a test to know if you have moved into perfectionism. Are you worried about your image? Are you working to assure others see your value?

Let your answers point you back toward the truth of your worthiness. We are not worthy because of what we have done. Because if you find any accolade and value in your successes, what happens when you fail? No matter how hard I worked in college, I was never the best in the class. My professional teaching accolades could not save the relationship when my first marriage ended. Success in the immediate is not a solution for long-term living.

My failures were always before me because I had rooted my worth in the feedback of those around me. If those I trusted saw my value, I thought it would secure my confidence. I worked for my worth because I believed it would cancel the missteps and bring me joy that had eluded me. However, we work from a place of worthiness when we accept the gift of God's grace and accept that we were made in his image.

● ● ●

When I hit rock-bottom, I was in my forties. You might think this was during my season of divorce, but it was actually years after that. I was buried under the heavy weight of proving my worth, a lifelong habit that came to a head when I stepped away from an unhealthy situation at church. What was motivating my striving became clear. Roles I assumed had given me temporary worth, but when they were stripped away, I did not know who I was. In that desert place, I began dismantling all the lies I had built my life on.

Accepting that my perfectionism was anchored to unworthiness was a healthy first step. The next was to pursue healing from past traumas. I had developed a love for order, a symptom of the pain of my unstable childhood, that showed up in doing good and being right. If I could prove my worth to others, maybe I would believe it myself.

One of the hardest lessons along my healing journey has been allowing myself to make mistakes. It was not until I ordered the wrong size phone case—a minor issue—that my intolerance for mistakes became clear. Two days after the case came in, I heard myself say something I had repeated several times already without thought. *I can't believe I ordered the wrong case.* What the heck? It was a simple mistake and not worth the time and fretting I was giving it. I began evaluating—as any good overthinker would—to determine the root of my fretting. It was perfectionism. The dreaded need for things to be right leaves no room for mistakes. This was my first lesson in allowing mistakes to take up residence in my life.

Please do not get me wrong on this. I had made innumerable mistakes throughout my life—massive mistakes at that—but I always worked to hide or correct those failures.

During a conversation with my therapist friend, she said something that gave me pause. After carrying on about how I could have handled my church hurt better, she pointed out my tendency to use a harsh lens with myself. Although the conversation continued, I was stuck on her previous words. When I asked her to clarify, she showed me how I made myself the problem in most situations. From her view, control was at the root. If I was the problem in situations, I could fix the problem. Do you hear the old familiar ring of needing to get things right? I was taking responsibility for any mistake because under it all was the limiting belief that I was a mistake. Framing mistakes as moral judgments against myself, instead of facts in my story, added shame too heavy to carry.

To make space for mistakes and to stop beating myself up for them was no simple task. Like the time last year when I called a meeting I forgot to attend. Seriously. We were in the throes of debriefing after a retreat our nonprofit hosted, and I assembled the team via Google Meet for the conversation. While they all gathered to wait for the virtual meeting to start, I was busy working in the kitchen. It was not until my co-founder sent me a text asking me where I was, and told me they were waiting for me online, that I remembered my obligation. The me of old would have apologized profusely for the error, but instead, I hopped online, smiled, and thanked everyone for their understanding. For the first time in a long time, I did not spend days beating myself up over the mistake.

While I am still on the healing path, I can tell you my load is lighter today. The bent toward perfectionism has not gone away, but it is no longer in the driver's seat. Recognizing that pain, perfectionism, and progress are planted in the same soil has given me direction when I am stuck in the weeds of life. Knowing which to cultivate requires wisdom born along the way. We get to choose what gets our attention, so we have more control than we may understand.

If certainty is knowing how to do something and confidence is knowing who you can depend on in the process, who do you lean on? Where do you turn when you need confidence? Who or what is the source of your confidence? There you will also find the essence of where your worthiness is rooted.

We were created for work, but that does not mean our worth comes from our success. When you reframe work in this way, it frees you to break up with perfectionism. Are you burned out from striving? It does not have to be that way. Get honest with yourself, find a professional to help you, and consider pursuing or deepening your faith. Maybe this is a new thought for you, but it is true. God delights in his children—even when no one else seems to. Tuck that truth in your pocket for the rest of your journey.

As you walk through the weeds of life, be sure to look for and collect gifts of wisdom along the way. They are there. Don't forget to put in the work to cultivate healthy roots to nourish your soul. Consider love as the antidote to perfectionism. Look for ways you can be kind and gentle with yourself. *Work from your worth, not for it.* When you decide to work from your worth, everything changes a little at a time.

When we take steps toward healing, we encounter the invitation to walk whole, walk tall, and walk worthy.

REFLECTION: Do you recognize any perfectionistic tendencies in your life? Till the soil to see where those might be rooted. If you are in a relationship with a perfectionist, consider ways you can extend the invitation of rest.

GOING DEEPER: Read Luke 12:6-7 and Isaiah 41:10. How do these passages interrupt your current patterns? Have you forgotten your value? How does God's nearness impact your worthiness? How does this challenge your perspective on perfectionism and worthiness?

Cultivating Surrender

Chapter Five

Broken to Grow

* Sometimes, things must be broken to be restored.

*"here is a strength, a power even, in under-
standing brokenness, because embracing our
brokenness creates a need and desire for mercy,
and perhaps a corresponding need to show mercy.
–Bryan Stevenson*

INSTEAD OF HEADING TO THE CAR, she shifted
direction and went straight for the flowerbed. Observ-
ing her movements, curious about the sudden pull
toward the plants, I was alarmed to see her bend
down and break the stem of one of the few living
plants in my humble garden. Mind you, said plant
resembled a stalk of harvested corn more than a living
organism.

In a panic, I bristled at her actions and questioned
her motive. Although I am not an adept gardener,
my mom is a wizard with plants. She knows when
to prune, how often to water, and the likes of such
plant-thriving necessities. I am sufficiently happy
when a plant survives a second week under my care.

While I wish that were an overstatement, it is not. Where my mom has plant intuition, I have zero.

My mom's ability in the garden substantiates her authority in decision-making. She has an established reputation as a good gardener, so why would I question her actions or defer to my own understanding? As she stooped low and snapped the stem, my confusion and distrust erupted in a statement laced with disbelief and indignation. *That plant is still living!* What my words lacked in snark, the question that followed delivered in full. *Why did you do that?*

Her answer surprised me. "I am breaking it so that it will grow back fuller." I saw death as an impending result of her actions; she saw the danger of the plant becoming tall and woody if left unpruned. In her experience, she knew breaking the stalk would encourage the plant to flourish. Though her reasoning felt counterintuitive, I could not stop ruminating on what she implied.

What appears perfectly fine is sometimes broken to promote fullness and growth. I had settled for a plant barely hanging on because I had no idea it could be healthier with a little intervention. I was content with the appearance of a thriving plant. While wrapping my head around that concept, I was struck by how that had also been true in my life experience. Because I have settled for the appearance of "good enough" in relationships with family, myself, and others, I did not fully understand how brokenness and hardship were strength-training opportunities where wisdom would emerge.

● ● ●

"Good enough" is an act of grace we extend to ourselves in challenging seasons. Sometimes good enough is our best foot forward, but when it becomes our permanent residence, we risk missing the abundance we were created to experience. Like the plant I would have allowed to shoot up and become woody, when we forget to make space for growth after the protective season of good enough, our full potential may be unrecognizable. We forget to prune criticism from conversation, turn the soil of compassion, and fertilize the roots of intimacy. We might defer to investing the bare minimum in primary relationships.

A good enough mindset is similar to simply *going through the motions.* You know what that looks like, right? Approaching tasks half-engaged, numb, and without passion. This happens for several reasons—burnout, distraction, exhaustion, defeat, and trauma. Sometimes the very best we can do is show up and go through the motions. It is one thing to survive a season by going through the motions and making soul concessions to show up in a good enough approach, but have you ever been guilty of permanently adopting this mentality?

Remaining in a disconnected approach to life after a time of brokenness and healing is a socially acceptable decision that few people will question. Maybe staying numb is easier than trusting the process of future healing and joy. Let's face it, healing takes time, and we are inclined to desire the immediate result. After my mom broke the stem of my barely-hanging-on plant, I did not see instant growth. Honestly, it was the next season before I saw any change. The timeline between brokenness and growth is not a one-size fits all formula. We cannot uproot from the source of life while we wait to see the evidence of growth; we have to fight the urge to check out and give up.

● ● ●

The other day, I was busy double-tasking. I was working on the computer and making lunch, so you could argue that I was going through the motions. Indulging one of the loves of my youth, I was cooking—rather—warming chicken nuggets in our toaster oven. The cooking time was 12 minutes, so I started them and returned to my work. I could hear the timer ticking gloriously toward lunch, so I walked away confident in the work of the toaster. When the timer went off, I reached in to take out the nuggets, which you know I was going to slather with Chick-fil-A sauce, and to my horror, they were still frozen. Upon closer investigation, I discovered the toaster was not plugged in. When I do not pause to assess my situation, I slide into a going through the motions mentality.

Much like a toaster cannot get power without being plugged in, and a flashlight will not work without batteries, plugging into the source always determines the outcome. It is not enough to be aware of how a toaster functions and what it is capable of. We have an obligation to plug into the power source to activate the full power of the appliance.

In the same way, our lives cannot thrive and grow to our fullest potential when we unplug from our true source of life. *Internal soul work takes a level of grit we cannot supply in our own strength.* When things get hard, the easiest decision is to throw in the towel. We need a source greater than our ability to traverse the steep inclines on the path through brokenness to growth.

I have gone through the motions, with an outward appearance of "fine", while my spirit withered from a lack of wellness and authentic connection. Can I be transparent? When I live like this, I am usually plugged into the source of my own understanding. Let me tell you, my record for leaning on my own knowledge is a losing one. Broken mirrors, false narratives, and illogical fears skew my assessments.

Maybe like me, you have spent a lot of energy walking around the brokenness and end up on paths that move away from healing, not toward it. We do not always see the value of investing in the work, so we find a way out. If we want to see fullness emerge from our brokenness, we must avoid getting out of what we need to get into. It may be time to disclose the hurt to a trusted friend, ask for help, or seek the wisdom of a mentor. When we face our wounds, instead of avoiding them, we give ourselves space to grieve. Those tears of grief water the soil and feed the roots of our souls. In an odd turn of events, our grief becomes the essence of what moves us from brokenness to growth.

● ● ●

Sleep, creep, and leap is a perennial plant theory that illustrates why we might struggle to wait. The first year of planting is known as the sleep year. While not actually sleeping, the plant works hard below the surface to establish a healthy root system necessary for the plant to flourish. This is the time when there is much waiting and anticipation, but the eye doesn't see significant growth. During year two, the plant will creep, and new foliage will grow that absorbs sunshine and fosters continued growth below the surface. Year three is known as the leap year. This is when significant growth and flourishing are obvious and pleasing to the eye.

Here's one observation from my own life. I desired year three of the plant theory moments after I planted in year one. If skipping from planting to flourishing was possible, would the plant be healthy? No. It is easy to desire a well-rooted, thriving plant and avoid the process of planting and germination. We are inclined to want the result, but as we wait, we discover that roots determine the fruit. Waiting is hard, but if we abandon the waiting process and lean on our understanding, we may miss the opportunity to be at our very best.

We want leap benefits like a tight-knit community of friends, but we also want to protect ourselves, so we withhold our exact needs and dreams. Bitter and brittle roots grow up in this soil. We want the healing and joy we see in someone else, but we have a million excuses why we won't go to counseling or ask for prayer. Jealous roots grow in this soil.

We assume brokenness is an indicator of our fatal errors as humans, but brokenness is a reminder of our humanity and deep need for our Creator. Many of us are guilty of covering up our brokenness or working harder to prove we can be better. We are varsity level at getting out of what we need to get into, and we wonder why life is dull.

Our Creator sees what our eyes cannot behold. What we see in part, God sees in whole. It is hard to trust a source you cannot touch, but if you simply watch the cycle of life, you see the Creator's planting, cultivating, pruning, and scattering process. It takes the entire process to propagate healing and hope. Although we often look for a way around pain and brokenness, discomfort is a part of the process. Growth is inevitable if we stick with the process through long days of waiting.

● ● ●

I would not have touched the plant my mom was drawn toward. It would have died slowly when the first freeze hit, and I would have crossed my fingers hoping for its return in the spring. Hope is powerful in the journey from brokenness to growth, but work must be coupled with hope in order to see healing. Hoping alone will not lead to growth.

My mom can assess a plant's growth trajectory at a glance. She does not hesitate to snap stems or deadhead flowers. Panic is not part of her process because she understands the order of living things. She knows that what a plant shows above the soil is connected to what is below the soil. Her years of practice provided wisdom.

The root will determine the fruit.

What I saw as living, she perceived room for growth. What I lacked in perspective, she had in abundance. A well-rooted plant will create new blooms. Brokenness is not the end. Let hope saturate the deep roots of your life, stay connected to your Creator, and be patient with the process.

Brokenness is bothersome. It is inconvenient, and it hurts. I am surprisingly good at avoiding painful things, so I am learning to look at my relationships with fresh eyes. Though not my instinct, I am warming up to the idea of being broken to be restored, to encourage fullness and new growth.

Sometimes, things must be broken to be restored.

Brokenness isn't the destination; it is a mile marker on the way to fullness if we stay the course. That may look like sitting in the tension of the brokenness without pretending we are okay and giving ourselves time, space, and grace to grieve the hurt. Growth is probable if we stick it out with our full commitment. We cannot go through the motions and get to abundance; we must consciously decide to take the path of healing.

I have replayed the garden scenario many times since the day it happened. Remembering that things must sometimes be broken to encourage new growth reminds me to lean in and trust the process, even when I cannot see or understand the purpose or possibility. What my eyes cannot see, I entrust to the Master Gardener and quiet my audible annoyance at the inconvenience of pain.

Pain is not the end of the story; it is the middle. There is more to come if we keep putting one foot in front of the other through our seasons of brokenness. The work is worth the reward.

Avoid the oppressive chokehold that avoidance offers. Let's get into the work of restoration bathed in hope. Give the process of moving through brokenness toward growth time. Abundance and fullness may be just around the corner. One day—not too far from now—your story of hope will be a guiding light for someone yet to understand the process. When you extend the mercy you found in the process, you provide fertilizer for the soil of someone else's journey through brokenness.

Just as the stem of a plant hardens as it ages, our unpruned hearts harden as hurt festers. Our experiences can make us bitter or better. Don't let fear keep you from moving toward healing. A beautiful garden born from the ashes of painful experiences is on the other side of our decision to stick it out. We may not do it perfectly, but we must keep moving forward.

REFLECTION: We are often driven to fix broken things or protect ourselves to avoid brokenness. Where does your brokenness drive you? Are you in the habit of self-preservation? What still needs time to heal in your life?

GOING DEEPER: Read Matthew 11:28-30 and John 7:37-38. What invitation is offered to broken, thirsty, and weary people?

Chapter Six

Even Though, Even When

* The tests we face are not indicators
of failure...

I can accept failure; everyone fails at something.
But I can't accept not trying.
–Michael Jordan

THINGS HAD NOT GONE according to plan. The knock at the door revealed the face of a perfect stranger with a suspicious smirk. He thrust a stack of papers in my direction, delivering a blow that knocked the wind out of my already tattered sails. Divorce papers were the catalyst of a dark and scary season. Being sued for sole custody of my two children, I found myself face down on the ground, wondering if I could take another breath.

Have you ever been frozen in a moment, wondering if life would ever be the same? Utter fear and sorrow paralyzed me; seeing beyond the storm was impossible, and hope was incalculable. Being a child of divorce, I was determined to shield my children from the painful memories I carried into adulthood.

To watch my resolve dissolve at the mercy of another's decision was a depth of trauma I had yet to know.

Already believing who I was, according to my insecurities, was wrong, I assumed the solution was to be better and do more to prove my worth. That burden is too heavy to bear and a price too great to pay. Layered loss skews truth in inarticulate ways that keep you fighting for a little evidence that you are not as disgusting as your wounds of failure declare. Weariness and disappointment short-circuit peace and impede clarity.

By the time I held the stack of legal papers in my hands, a world of ideas and dreams had long been abandoned. The little girl in me had learned to reach for being right over all else. She associated being right and being good with being loved. She swallowed warnings, stuffed insight, and settled for avoiding trouble by flying under the radar. She learned to shrink back and entertain an unparalleled loneliness which confirmed her suspicion that she was not worth seeing or loving.

That little girl became a young mother confronted with broken dreams, altered plans, and unresolved wounds. Because I believed the evidence of failures in my life was more significant than my potential, I stopped trying to prove I was good. Even before the divorce papers, the message was repeatedly confirmed by the narrative of my childhood and young adult experiences. Compounded with layered trauma, a skewed perspective of my worth kept a tight grip on me for many years. Fear routinely shouted at me to sit down, be silent, and try harder, but no matter how much I tried, I could not find my way to peace. I could not control the outcome or craft the perfect life, but oh, how I tried.

● ● ●

Although things have not gone according to my best laid plans, ever, this is familiar in the annals of history. I was comforted by the narrative of one of the great patriarchs of the Bible, Abraham. His life, calling, and promise were filled with shifting sands and altered plans. Those were two things woven into the backdrop of my life, so his story felt like the solidarity I needed in the cloudiest season of my life.

Abraham was called from the familiarity of his life to go to a new land, but he was not given an exact blueprint. He was called from his familiar before he knew where his journey would lead. There was a palpable tension in my shoulders as I thought about the space between his now and not yet, and mine.

What struck me is how he responded to the tension. Genesis 12:4 says, "So Abram left..." He had a ready-obedient response when he was called despite the lack of information and step-by-step instructions.

My own tendency is to respond with resistance when things do not make sense, yet here was an older man getting on board with only scraps of information.

Abraham is later told that he will be the father to many nations, but it is worth noting that he was married to a barren woman. That had to leave room for doubt, cynicism, and a thousand other feelings, yet he believed and obeyed. After many years of waiting, his wife becomes pregnant and gives birth to a son who Abraham will be asked to sacrifice. For. Real.

You will have to check out the remainder of that story on your own, but trust me when I say his response reveals a character of consistency. With no itinerary or tangible assurance negotiated in advance, Abraham willingly moved forward with a blurry, at best, plan.

Hebrews 11:8-11 provides an account of his agreement.

"By faith Abraham, when called to go to a place he would later receive as his inheritance, obeyed and went, *even though* he did not know where he was going. By faith he made his home in the promised land like a stranger in a foreign country; he lived in tents, as did Isaac and Jacob, who were heirs with him of the same promise. For he was looking forward to the city with foundations, whose architect and builder is God. And by faith even Sarah, who was past childbearing age, was enabled to bear children because she considered him faithful who had made the promise." [emphasis mine]

Even though is a phrase I had not considered until I read this passage. When used as a conjunction, it strongly emphasizes the contrast between the two connecting phrases. Abraham obeyed even though he did not know where he was going. Since he did not have the benefit of GPS or even an ancient blueprint of the destination, questions and curiosity undoubtedly filled his mind.

As if that was not enough, he also waited 25 years to see the promise of an heir. I struggle to wait 25 minutes for a returned phone call, email, or text message. Can you imagine the stamina he showed in the waiting? In the face of it all, he kept walking. He continued to put one foot in front of the other and waited expectantly. He believed even though the isolated, individual pieces of instruction did not add up to anything tangible. He acted in obedience even when he did not have clarity.

● ● ●

Walking through a divorce was not what I had planned, but it also did not end my life. The custody battle was painful and expensive, and I would not wish it on anyone. Full stop. Sitting alone and crying became my new normal. Being called into an all-out war for my life was definitely the worst of all the hard things in my life.

Existing in the context of divorce was not unfamiliar since my parents separated when I was ten, but it knocked the wind out of me when it became my story. Questions moved in because my identity was suddenly hanging in the balance. Who I thought I was—the value I assumed I brought to the table—had crumbled instantly. Who was I now? Was I still qualified to volunteer at church? Would it be weird to hang out with the same friends? Where would I "fit" now that I was single and a mom? Who were my people?

Moving forward was made possible by holding firm to my faith. I did not know if I could rebuild my life, but I trusted God would not leave me alone in the battle. Like a house thrashed by a tornado ripping through, I began sifting through the rubble of my life to determine if anything valuable could be salvaged. I snagged a few things I thought might be helpful in the next season, but I endeavored to let most of it go. Rebuilding without faith would have looked more like a renovation that ran out of funding, but with faith, it looked more like a restoration. Keeping the integrity of my heart meant the process would be tedious and slow, but learning to stay present in each moment was its own kind of treasure hunt.

Seasons of transition are tough to navigate because the unknown often gives birth to anxiety. This chapter in my life was no exception. I cried more tears than I can count during my "renaming" season—when I moved from finding my identity as a married woman to a single mother. Sometimes, my tears were driven by fear. Other times, my tears came from anger over being blindsided by divorce or someone's innocent inquiry about the kids when they had been away on a visit for what felt like weeks. The pain, the longing, and the sadness were a lot, and I knew I had zero control over anything. My world tilted upside down, and I had no choice but to unfurl my hands and lay all my longings down.

Surrendering control did not cause my tears to cease from flowing, but I discovered feeling like a mess mattered very little in the process. Authenticity mattered, so I began telling God about the depth of my disappointment. As I took baby steps in healing, I sensed a redefining slowly taking place. My heart opened to the idea of being reborn as a whole woman. Even when I was holding the pieces of shattered dreams…even though I did not know how the children and I would survive, we did. I got up every day and did the next right thing even when I was fighting mad, even though the story of my life took a turn I did not anticipate.

God is at work in the *even though, even when* moments of our lives. At least it is where He wants to work if we are willing to surrender our doubts, fears, insecurities, and questions and believe that something better is possible. The tests we face are not indicators of failure; they provide pathways away from fear even when we do not know exactly where they will lead.

The tension in our unknowns is glorious and messy. It is the intersection of anguish and hope. *Even though* is where our faith is built and put to the test. It is often in the weeds of the middle place, where things have not been resolved and are not yet understood, that lessons of wisdom emerge. We learn to believe even when we don't understand the plan. Faith and hope collide in that space, and a story of courage and tenacity is born where fear once held us captive.

REFLECTION: What is your even though in this season of your life? What are you moving through despite the unknown?

GOING DEEPER: Read Proverbs 3:5-6. What is holding you back from taking steps of active faith?

Chapter Seven

Forcing, Waiting, and Other Elementary Lessons

* Desire intensifies the weight of waiting.

To dig for treasures shows not only impatience and greed, but lack of faith…one should lie empty, open, choiceless as a beach-waiting for a gift from the sea.
—*Anne Morrow Lindbergh, Gift from the Sea*

Forcing a blessing IS AN INABILITY to see beyond the moment—the carrot dangling before us. The decision to reach earnestly for what is desired with unrelenting determination. Stepping back and gaining a broader perspective would take too much time, discipline, and waiting. You may understand this deep in your core. Maybe you stepped into a relationship to circumvent loneliness, but your "yes" created a tension of deep dissatisfaction in your soul. Maybe you said yes to that job because it seemed like the only option, but it ended up creating problems you are still unraveling. Maybe you compromised your integrity for a moment of fleeting fulfillment, and the repercussions of that decision continually remind you of your lapse of judgment and aggravate a silent sense of failure.

Our lack of vision for the future is attached to our inability to trust in the present. We struggle to trust ourselves and others because we have been disappointed, and if we can avoid feeling that way again, we will do whatever it takes. This feeds the fiercely independent spirit living inside us. We will get what we want when we want it, and no one has access to counsel us otherwise. Thank you very much.

● ● ●

My neighbor is a fierce animal advocate. She has bird feeders, deer feeders, and stray anything feeders. She is the one you call when your dog is sick, or there is a lizard trapped under your bookshelf, but you don't have a pet lizard. She is generous and gentle in equal measure. In an act of generosity, she once brought a block of birdseed over to our house, and we felt so proud to join the ranks of those loving yard creatures.

Between our houses, we have several large resident squirrels. It didn't take long to grow frustrated with one squirrel who regularly hung upside down from the tree to feast on our newly placed birdseed block. He would scare the birds off when they landed by lunging from his perch in the tree. I would run out like a maniac whenever I caught him on the feeder, but it was useless. He won the persistence trophy.

One day, I watched the squirrel straddle a small bird feeder in my neighbor's yard. He pounded away at the small opening, enjoying anything that fell out. I was aghast at his bad manners and disregard for the obvious rule against stealing food from a friend's plate. As I shamed the squirrel, I couldn't help but wonder about the root of my indignation. The thought occurred to me—in that moment—how much I am just like that squirrel. I get caught up in what others have, the gifts they have been given, the blessings I see pour out on them, and I want the same for myself.

What I didn't like about the squirrel was what I don't like about me. I become a squirrel pillaging bird feeders when I fail to appreciate and steward my lot in life and labor over manipulating situations to get even the tiniest reward. I sat down on my rocking chair and recognized the countless times I had been and continue to be a squirrel on a bird feeder, and the times I have forced blessings I thought were rightly mine.

On the other side of my neighbor's house was a squirrel feeder. If that stubborn squirrel had gone there, his meal would have required less effort. Because he was short-sighted and impatient, he settled for crumbs. Forcing the blessing does that; it breaks treasures, provides a less fulfilling meal, and sacrifices what's best for what is first. Desire intensifies the weight of waiting.

● ● ●

When our children were young, we liked sprinkling surprises into the ordinary duties of our lives. One of the cheapest ways to do that was to hit Sonic for Happy Hour drinks. Without fail, my husband and I would have just planned to stop when one of the kiddos would begin a petition to go to Sonic. I cannot make this up. The plea would include all the reasons why it made sense to indulge in a treat, and we obviously agreed because we had planned to stop. Something about the insistence robbed us of the joy of the surprise, and we wondered why they could not wait on our blessing.

Our youngest spotted a Lego book at Target that set his heart aflame. He was not one to let something go quickly, so he launched into a full-blown tantrum when we told him we would not buy it. As we walked toward the exit, he could be heard throughout the store saying "I need that." Little did he know that we had already made eyes about one of us running back in to purchase the book for his Easter basket. Trading the best thing for the first thing looks a little like stomping our foot until we get our way.

Waiting is excruciating. Anxiety in the waiting rises to a level that causes us to make decisions that mandate sacrifices unseen. When one digs for a treasure at the beach, the unseen sacrifice could well be breaking a beautiful shell or sand dollar. In impatience, I am guilty of sacrificing the best for what is first.

During a family beach vacation, I witnessed a tangible lesson in the value of waiting. I arrived at my beach chair with just enough time to see my husband and oldest son escape into the distance in search of a sand dollar. I could see them crouch down and move their hands through the soupy sand before continuing. They were immersed in conversation while working toward a common goal. Hours passed before they returned to our beach house with the sweetest grin and the joy of a story they couldn't keep to themselves.

Each time they explored the shore, they unearthed broken pieces of sand dollars they referred to as "change". My son beamed as he recalled the decision to keep each broken sand dollar and how they'd gathered an impressive amount of change throughout the day. My guys were motivated, however, to continue looking for a whole sand dollar. Unfortunately, as their stamina waned, disappointment grew. At my husband's initiation, they threw all the pieces back into the ocean. As they deposited the pieces in the rolling waters, they audibly asked God if they could give Him change for a dollar. At that, they gave up their treasure hunt and began the long walk back toward the house.

When they were nearly halfway home, they just so happened to stumble across a whole sand dollar. It was in plain sight, untouched…a blessing waiting to be received. No forcing or digging is necessary.

That's the heart I desire. Too often I am more like a child in the throes of a temper tantrum. Fists and feet banging away at the disappointment of not getting what I wanted. Waiting takes discipline and hope. Like the quote at the beginning of the chapter, I want to wait for a gift from the sea and a meal intended for me—the blessing God desires to lavish on me.

Waiting, in a world with answers revealed with one click, is an act of discipline and trust. The challenge for me is that I rarely strike a balance between the two. With my stringent personality, I can be highly disciplined with a trust tethered to myself but trusting in myself is a hopeless prospect. I know me. Trusting in something bigger and stronger than my understanding makes more sense, but I inevitably lean on my own understanding in my impatience.

● ● ●

An early memory of trusting my own plan instead of waiting haunts me to this day. The classroom was dark; my classmates played outside before the morning bell initiated the start of the day. Creeping into the room, I headed straight for my teacher's desk.

There I found a small box containing paper cutouts of boys and girls. I rifled through the cutouts until I found the one with my name. With my heart beating wildly and my eyes on the door, I tip-toed over to the bulletin board announcing the new student of the week, gently removed the cutout already pinned in place, and replaced it with the one bearing my name. It was my turn.

Swelling with pride in my accomplishment and anxiety at being found out, I knew I had pulled off the greatest heist in history. Since my history only included 312 or so weeks, I didn't have much in the way of comparison. I stealthily returned outside and waited for the call of the bell.

Entering the classroom, I held my head high and tried to act like everything was normal, but nothing was. I felt the weight of my sweet teacher's gaze. The knowing look tracked me around the room. Maybe I liked that. Maybe I was desperate for more than the opportunity to be the line leader. Maybe what I really wanted was to be noticed by forcing her attention.

She never addressed my blatant trespass that day and allowed me to assume the dignity of being the student of the week, the greatest position for an over-achieving student. She made space for this forced favor, even though, in hindsight, it is clear she knew what I had done. It's not as though she mindlessly chose the student of the week that morning. For it to

93

suddenly be changed was not an unexpected miracle; it was a deliberate act by a desperate little girl.

She had every right to address the matter with me. She could have humiliated me before my peers, but she didn't. I had acted according to what I wanted; I had not waited my turn. I had forced an experience; I hadn't trusted her timeline or plan. I was in first grade, but this would become a pattern I repeated many times in the years that proceeded.

My teacher extended something to me that I didn't deserve, unmerited favor. She saw my failure as an opportunity. She looked beyond my behavior and into my heart. She made a deposit in my life that I still carry with me. I did not get what I deserved; I got something I didn't deserve. She left my heart intact even when I forced a blessing. Because she saw me and saw beyond my behavior, I had the privilege of learning how to extend grace by receiving hers that day.

We can give the gift of grace to someone in our lives. We can seek reconciliation. We can let go of an offense. We can pump the brakes on the thing we have been forcing. It is never too late to start over, say we are sorry, and begin again.

My counselor told me that her culture values letting problems figure themselves out. That is counterintuitive in a culture that prides itself on problem-solving. She invited me to practice not caring so much by allowing moments to unfold without my intervention. She encouraged me to give up being a squirrel on a birdfeeder. She suggested I open my eyes to see the provision set out just for me.

Our lack of vision for the future is attached to our inability to trust in the present. What might happen if we lean less on our own understanding and more on trusting the divine plan of our Creator? We have not been forgotten. Feel the weight of waiting. We are not too late. There is enough for us. Feel free to climb off the birdfeeder and find the provision that is uniquely yours. It's there. Keep your eyes open.

When we are in the weeds, we are inclined to tighten our grip around the things we think are within our control. We let panic drag us toward what is first instead of what is best. The practice of waiting is more than an elementary lesson; it is a lesson for here and now. Will we let it unfold?

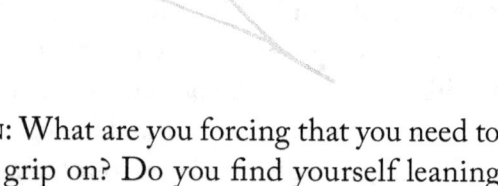

REFLECTION: What are you forcing that you need to loosen your grip on? Do you find yourself leaning more on your own understanding or trusting the nature of your Creator?

GOING DEEPER: Read John 3:16-17 and Psalm 40:1-4. What motivated the grace we have been offered? What will you do with the gift of unmerited favor?

Chapter Eight

The Power of the Pivot: Lessons We Didn't Know We Needed to Learn

* There is wisdom to be found in the
  weeds. Stick it out.

*I always get to where I'm going by walking
away from where I have been.*
—Winne the Pooh

THOUGH I FELT EAGER FOR 2019 TO END, I cannot remember exactly why. It is the nature of my personality to anticipate ways things could be better, so it makes sense that I was looking ahead instead of remembering the days behind. Who could have known what the days ahead would hold? The year I thought held the promise of abundance started by teaching me to stop and ultimately learn a lesson I didn't know I needed.

Quarantine was a whole new way of life. Fear of the unknown was palpable, and the lockdown honeymoon wore off sooner than I expected. I craved a quick return to normal, so when a few weeks of the stay-at-home order turned into more, there were only two options—pout or pivot. I tried the first to no avail, so I opted to pivot out of necessity.

The power of the pivot is gaining a different perspective. I could stare at the obstacle or look for a new opportunity. It turns out that the difference between a bankrupt and an abundant outlook is perspective.

Adjusting my work life required heavy-lifting. I was overwhelmed with moving an entire school online in a matter of a few days. Because of the uncharted territory, the task made me feel physically and emotionally bankrupt. Teaching live classes while my children filled their metal water bottles with one million ice cubes was annoying, but their presence was also a gift. I had to learn the quick draw mute skill and remember how to laugh off minor disturbances.

When the Wi-Fi lagged because our house was the unofficial headquarters of "Zoom University", my first instinct was to point the finger of blame and elevate my needs over everyone else's. With a tiny pivot, I saw the courageous way my children were also navigating a whole new world. I recognized the need to affirm their efforts and stop fussing about the bandwidth. Everyone was learning how to thrive in a new reality. A tiny pivot changed my perspective of the inconvenience.

We cannot grab onto the lovely while clutching the horrible. When our hands do not let go of the gross, they cannot grab hold of the good. Renewed hope is made possible by the perspective birthed in the pivot. Otherwise, discouragement and fear of the same become the filter through which we view everything else, and we no longer lean into expectancy. The incalculable gift of having my family under one roof was not something I understood at the onset of lockdown, but a tiny pivot sparked an inexplicable hope in my heart. It had been years since all the chairs were occupied around our table.

To pivot, we must turn from one thing toward another while holding our position with one foot planted firmly on the ground. The only problem with the pivot is remembering to keep a foot on the floor. My instinct is to see trouble and run toward safety or crumble to the ground in the fetal position. The pivot is about stance and strength. What happens when we apply a strong position over our difficulties by keeping our feet planted on the ground in the face of trouble? Let's consider the buffalo to answer that question.

You may already know this, but the buffalo's instinct is to run into a storm. On the contrary, a cow sees a storm and runs away from it. Running away serves to dodge the storm, but it doesn't eliminate it. Running into the storm, or standing in a strong position despite the storm, is where suffering becomes a story of hope and endurance. We are guaranteed to endure difficulties in this life; they are as inevitable as the sun's rising and setting. How we engage the challenges is a decision left entirely to us. I want to be like the buffalo in the face of the storm, but my instinct is to avoid painful things by running away. When things get hard, I am learning to change my perspective by pivoting. There is always another way to look at an experience.

● ● ●

Although I was born and raised in Illinois, I moved to Texas to complete my student teaching experience. It felt like a study abroad opportunity that carried a smaller price tag. I expected tumbleweeds, cowboys, and lots of wide-open spaces. While I wish I could tell you I am exaggerating, I most certainly am not. Not only had I never visited Texas, I did not do a lick of research before packing up my measly belongings to begin my new adventure.

What caught me by surprise, besides the fact that the Alamo is located smack dab in the middle of downtown, was the amount of gorgeous wildflowers that appeared in the spring. Texas boasts fields of stunning flowers in various colors, including the Bluebonnet, which begins to bloom in early March.

Unfortunately, my first experience with Bluebonnets left me wanting. Let me explain. I had not been living in Texas long when my mom and sister came for a visit. We were driving along a back road in the Hill Country when we decided to pull off and take a picture in the wildflowers. For those who are not Texan, pictures in wildflowers always retain their popularity here. Google "bluebonnet pictures of kids or families" for a better understanding.

We made our way to a brilliant patch of flowers, smiled pretty, and hopped back in the car to head home. As we were pulling away, I felt something stinging me. It was a discomfort like nothing I had ever experienced. When I looked down to see what was going on, I was befuddled. To my surprise and horror, a few ants were crawling on top of my foot, and they were biting me. Ants. And that was the moment I discovered that fire ants were a thing. Until that day, I had zero clue that ants could bite. After being here for a few decades, I have learned to thoroughly inspect a grassy area *before* taking a step forward because fire ants are *absolutely* a thing, and stepping into a fire ant pile is a horrid experience.

My introduction to fire ants taught me to pay attention, but it also revealed another life lesson; *unexpected and painful things can live just below the surface of beautiful things.*

● ● ●

I grew up as the youngest of three girls. My home life was marked by some traumatic experiences. At the time, I would have only been able to tell you that I felt afraid and alone. When the tension grew thick, I would retreat to the twelve inches of space between my bed and the floor. People could not see the pain I lugged around under the surface of my smile because I learned to hide from difficulties. I developed the belief that flying under the radar would keep me safe, and safety was my priority.

The idea of pivoting from fear never crossed my mind. Surviving emotional landmines in a war zone requires adaptations a child cannot fully realize or understand. My response was to hide and avoid, and because of that, I learned to exist in voicelessness, which birthed a limited perspective. Think about how your visibility changes when you cover your eyes. When you are confined literally or metaphorically to a dark, tight space, there is little you can do to adjust your vantage point. As a child, the idea of pivoting would have to be demonstrated by a trusted adult, but we were surviving, so I did not learn the power of the pivot.

Being unable to hold my position or keep a foot anchored to the ground left me disoriented. I spent many years comfortably uncomfortable in my trauma because it was all I had ever known. The work of healing and true transformation would eventually come with a pivot and perspective shift. It would take intentional work for several years to have compassion for my younger self, to recognize opportunities to face my storms instead of employing my avoidance instinct, and to understand the gift of empathy and wisdom born from the experiences of trauma.

Can I take a minute to level the playing field? Often when people hear the word trauma, their understanding is limited to veterans of war and PTSD. Dr. Anita Phillips defines trauma as "anything that has changed your view of God, the world, others, or yourself for the worse—in a way that shook you deeply."[6] Let that ruminate for a minute.

Trauma is not limited to them and when; it is also a challenge for us and now.

We are all impacted in some way by experiences that changed us for the worse. It is wise to pay attention to how we respond to storms and what may be just below the surface of our actions.

Voicelessness fed my tendency toward feeling afraid, lonely, lost, and unsure about the smallest details. I lived many years trying to do enough to be seen and valued. I made decisions from a wounded and scared place, not a place of love. I worked my tail off, but I was on a never-ending treadmill—working and getting nowhere.

My exhaustion was overwhelming, and a need to pivot bubbled up in me. I needed healing, but I was afraid to go to counseling because I thought needing counseling confirmed my deeply ingrained belief that who I was was wrong. Before I said "yes" to counseling, I was given an opportunity to attend a Life Plan retreat. The coaching company defined the retreat with the following words.

REKINDLE YOUR PASSIONS.
DISCOVER YOUR PURPOSE.
LIVE DIFFERENTLY.

I was like, YES! For someone who had struggled to know what she wanted, this was something I immediately knew I needed. I had work I was supposed to do beforehand, yet I still somehow managed not to prepare my heart for the dramatic change that was about to unfold. Although slightly tentative, I packed my bags and headed to the weekend retreat.

When you fly under the radar, you keep things as smooth as possible. No ripples. No waves. That decision led me to a life of utter dullness. Even in my faith, I recognized my quick response to serve and do, and my hesitancy to sit, be, and receive. I had learned to not have needs and to negotiate my position instead of holding my stance. Then Life Plan happened. I sat face to face with the truth that I was living a boring story. I was living a boring story in the shallow end of my faith because it was safe. It was easier for me to believe that safety was best because my narrative was full of evidence that pointed to that truth.

During one retreat session, we were sent out to be quiet, to consider all we had uncovered throughout the weekend, and write a legacy letter to ourselves. The pump had been primed to let words of purpose and encouragement pour out of me to me. Here are the words I wrote to the lost little girl and battle-weary woman.

Dear Alyssa,

You've seen God move mountains and make a way where you saw no way possible. It has been easy for you to lose sight of provision because fear bullied you into keeping inventory of what you lacked.

A good home life doesn't qualify you. Holding it all together and getting it all right won't qualify you. Jesus did that when he knit you together in your mother's womb.

He knew what family and resulting circumstances you would endure. He never meant for you to figure it out—to cut a pathway through your pain. Though unseen, God was never removed from your moment by moment existence. You assumed a life when he wanted to take you further.

That dream of being a lawyer—it wasn't too big or beyond you. But you settled for something less because it was easier for you to imagine and make happen. Stop trusting your own resources. Put your trust in God. He alone created you; he alone can sustain you. Will you believe that—not as more head knowledge, but as a radical life-changing truth?

You are done living the mediocre life. Stop settling for boring. Status quo is not the abundance you were created for. You are content with scraps when storehouses await you.

Let yourself go in your relationships. Remove the fence of failure. Remove the life vest. Jump in. Splash around in the lives entrusted to you. Make passion— not pessimism—your pursuit. Love hard and big without the prospect of return on investment.

Hope is your driver. Let the car out of park and get going. Your ideas are not silly. The world needs your brand of creative kindness. Don't be content sitting in silence. The kindness project. Invite others into it. Your story. Tell it. That book. Write it.

Seek the Lord—your provider. He has rich and glorious things to tell you. You are approved. Please believe this. Trust God with the unfolding of your plans. He is working on, in, and through you. You are free to color outside the lines and pursue creative interests. Just don't forget to write the story—all of it.

You matter, Alyssa. Always.

This letter was a turning point. I had lived in seasons where predictable was my most coveted dream. Predictable doesn't create space for a pivot. Both feet are planted, and perspective is fixed in the pursuit of the safety of predictability. I was ready to see my life differently, but the process would be complicated. It is easy to want the result and begrudge the process. I am guilty of wanting to jump from the start to the finish line or giving up on a dream when obstacles appear. Talk about short-sightedness.

● ● ●

As a child, I spent an inordinate amount of time at the dentist. I can not be sure if I was always the one receiving treatment or if I was just along for the ride, but I was well-acquainted with the office. The receptionist had a sign on her desk that intrigued me. It was like a stereograph where you stare at an image until the hidden picture emerges. The sign on her desk was made of two colors of wood. I always focused on light colors, and my eyes beheld utter nothingness. In my frustration, I would quit by convincing myself I didn't really care, but the truth is, I desperately wanted to see what everyone else could see.

Sticking it out means putting in long hours. It means considering the pivot between quitting and persisting. Sometimes we need a little coaching to know how to effectively use the power of the pivot. On one of my trips to the dentist, the hygienist encouraged me to adjust my perspective. She said to focus on the dark wood instead of the light pieces. With one small adjustment, the entire world opened, and the hidden message was as clear as day. *Hello.*

Life Plan was not a standard retreat; it was a coaching opportunity. Coaching requires vulnerability and trust. It was time to let my guard down and learn to trust the process. I was ready to pull up and start flying above the radar. This shifted my vantage point and invited me to lean into expectancy.

● ● ●

Corrie ten Boom, a woman who, with the help of her sister, looked at the awful experience of being imprisoned for harboring Jews, sleeping in flea-infested bunks, and other unthinkable experiences as an opportunity. In her book, The Hiding Place, she shares her belief that God uses all our experiences as preparation for the work he will give us.[7]

I would not have chosen childhood trauma as my story. The work of healing has been tedious and dang hard. Every day I have a choice to worship the hurt or honor the Healer, and I don't always make the better choice. Even amid the uphill climb, I see the gift of empathy and wisdom born in the soil of pain. The hurt doesn't have the final say. Without the battle, I would not have gained ground to exercise compassion with others.

This is the power of the pivot. It is letting go of the pain of hardships to lay hold of future possibilities. It is the decision to hold your stance, shift slightly, and gain a new perspective. We can stare at the obstacle or look for the opportunity. It turns out that the difference between a bankrupt outlook, focusing solely on the losses in our lives, and an abundant outlook, the opportunities born out of trials, is perspective. How we see our experiences impacts the lessons we collect. There is always an alternate perspective than the one we tend toward, but we have to work to consider it.

Don't try to jump straight to the finish line on this one. Let baby steps toward strengthening your pivot foot be enough. Consider one circumstance at a time. Look for hope among the ruins of past situations. There is wisdom to be found in the weeds. Stick it out. When the storm comes, use your pivot foot to turn toward it. You have what you need to grab hold of the lesson sprouting from fertile soil drenched by the unexpected rain.

REFLECTION: How have you responded to life's difficulties? Are you open to exercising the power of pivoting? We don't have to be overwhelmed by turning everything around; we can choose to live one day better than the last. It is easier to visualize change when we consider it one decision at a time. What one decision can you make today? Commit to taking one step forward.

GOING DEEPER: Read Psalm 34. What is the implied pivot in this passage? Do you sense that the pivot birthed a perspective change? What is the hope among the ruins?

Chapter Nine

Learning to Unlearn

* Transformation is always worth the investment.

Transformation is often more about unlearning than learning.
—*Richard Rohr*

HAVE YOU EVER CONSIDERED the bedrock of your long-held beliefs? Where and how did you learn some of your deepest convictions? A few years ago, I walked through a trying time. The ground beneath me felt unsteady as things I had always known as "right" began to unravel, and I was thrust into a season of transformation. *Who told you that* became a checkpoint question on my journey of dismantling and rebuilding.

When my first marriage unraveled, I believed I was no longer allowed to volunteer at church.

When my plate was too full to say yes to one more good thing, I believed I was a disappointment.

When I felt dismissed by a leader I admired, I believed my voice was unnecessary.

Who told me that? Where did I learn that?

It is all around us. You see it and feel it, right? Wear this brand, drive that car, live in this neighborhood or area of town, have children, sign them up for all the things to ensure future success, and be sure to have incredible social media posts to prove how well things are going. Innumerable influences are selling us information, but what they are selling (and we are routinely buying) is not always true. I have found myself believing subtle distortions of the truth without even recognizing when or how they emerged.

Pausing and practicing the phrase *who told you that?* has been the key to unlocking a prison of false narratives. I started making a list in one of my journals of particular personal convictions that had been part of my repertoire for so long. Not only did I not know where they originated, I had never questioned their validity or credibility. As I began examining each one, I understood that many of my beliefs were rooted in someone else's conviction or steeped in tradition. I had not paused long enough to consider what I thought about the topics. This awareness triggered a lengthy season of dismantling where I had to learn to unlearn patterns set and cured in my soul, but in the process, I experienced transformation. One of the areas requiring acute attention was the way I looked for evidence of my value. Because I desperately wanted to be valued, I rarely exercised my "no." Without healthy boundaries, I became like an old pair of socks that lost their elasticity. The stretching left my life sagging under the pressure of doing, but not necessarily feeling valuable.

● ● ●

My attendance was routine. My allegiance was unwavering. Everything was functioning just as it should—until it wasn't. For as long as I can remember, church played a significant role in my life. If the doors were open, my family was somewhere inside, so it should come as no surprise the practice carried into my adult life.

When stormy seasons hit, my church family steadied me. My small group brought gifts and sang with gusto when my children had birthdays. When loneliness smothered my joy, mentors and friends filled the void with hopeful declarations over my life. This connection was the foundation of my identity, the sinews of my soul. However, there was a subtle shift in my loyalties somewhere along the way. An imbalance between love and duty threw my motivations into a tailspin.

As ministry opportunities and responsibilities grew, I elevated my roles over the benefits of my relationship with the Lord. If someone asked me to lead a group or speak at an event, I collected the invitation as evidence of my worth. I tethered my identity to the responsibility, not to Jesus. Anything elevated above the adoration of Jesus is idolatry. The last thing I would have called myself was idolatrous. Church, after all, is a good thing, but blurred lines become burdens.

Jeremiah 2:13 says, "For My people have committed two evils: they have forsaken Me, the fountain of living waters, and hewn themselves cisterns—broken cisterns that can hold no water."

Cisterns were artificial reservoirs created to hold water. They were a manufactured holding tank where water didn't naturally rise. The necessity of creating a space to store water met a primal need. When a cistern cracked, it allowed impurities to infiltrate the water and render it undrinkable, and the cracks also allowed water to escape into the surrounding soil. Consequently, broken cisterns become contaminated and eventually run dry.

Serving at church was a broken cistern where I went regularly to find and confirm my identity. No matter how many times I looked for my value in saying yes, my thirst for truth was never satisfied. *My worth was entangled with my service.* I did not see the blurred boundaries. How could a good thing be wrong? This was what I had known for most of my life. What I had yet to calculate was that I was using the role to prove my worth. Untangling worth from service was no simple task.

Sometimes trials hit like unexpected summer storms. This was certainly true as I began feeling the nudge to set boundaries with my "yes" and move away from finding my value in being at every meeting, sitting on every committee, and being a part of the behind-the-scenes planning. None of those decisions by themselves were bad. Where things went sideways for me was not being able to differentiate good from guilt and reasonable from ridiculous. Saying yes to one thing means saying no to another, but saying no to something is also saying yes to something else. I had to practice exercising my no.

Have you ever had a necklace intermingle with another? It is frustrating to untangle the jumbled mess. I might be the person who ends up pulling so hard every necklace breaks. I might also be the person who throws the whole entangled mess away, but I am also the person who knows that someone else is good at correcting the mess. My husband has methodically rescued many necklaces from my wrath. He patiently pulls and works one tangle at a time until he recovers the individual chains. I want things to be fixed right away. He knows the result will take time.

● ● ●

Dismantling was not my desire but a necessary detour in my story. Unlearning is like untangling. It takes time to inspect the source of the knot—the thing you have built an entire life around. It takes determined effort to separate one strand from another. Sifting through what is helping and what is hurting is cumbersome, and calculating the emotional toll of change is nearly impossible. It is hard work to hold on to what is good while releasing what is unnecessary, and sometimes we miss the best things in life because we settle for the easiest path.

After examining our motives, my husband and I decided to step outside our comfort zone and chase our faith into the unknown. We had to believe that the next thing would provide exactly what we needed, even though the evidence had yet to be seen. We were *being called from* the church we had attended for many years without knowing where we were *being called to*. This seemed like the absolute opposite of a logical decision, and I love logic.

Have you heard the phrase refiner's fire? "A refiner's fire does not destroy indiscriminately like a forest fire. A refiner's fire does not consume completely like the fire of an incinerator. A refiner's fire purifies. It melts down the bar of silver or gold, separates out the impurities that ruin its value, burns them up, and leaves the silver and gold intact."[8]

Fire purifies gold and silver. The purpose of the refiner's fire is not destruction but development. The treasure was always present; the fire simply enhanced the value.

Our life experiences are not exempt from facing fires. Some fiery trials will burn off the things that have weighed us down and held us back; other times of enduring the fire will strengthen us for our ultimate purpose. If we endure the heat, lessons of strength, durability, and wisdom emerge. While we may find ourselves uncomfortable for a season, the ultimate gift is an enhanced perspective and reoriented hope.

Although unaware, my husband and I were entering a long season of refining. When you walk away from a longstanding relationship, it is messy. Not everyone was happy; people felt disappointed and abandoned by our decision to leave our community of faith to chase purpose outside the lines of what was familiar. The greatest lesson I learned in the fire was this-hard things don't have to be harsh, and difficult things don't have to be destructive. We could leave our friends without losing our faith. We could endure the hard season without criticizing all our friends who stayed. The fire is meant to mature our faith, not become a weapon to destroy others. Unlearning unhealthy patterns was the conduit of deep transformative work in the secret places of my soul because the fire was inviting me to a deeper personal and spiritual maturity.

My refining included an awareness that the context of my confidence had been my knowledge, my abilities to speak and lead, and my discernment. I was drinking from a broken cistern of volunteerism because I thought that would bring security. That is a hard truth to face. I did not want to admit the trial of leaving church was rooted in idolatry driven by insecurity. Sometimes you have to walk away from what is familiar to find out what truly matters.

A part of dismantling we forget to consider is that things must be torn down before they can be rebuilt. My husband and I lost friends. We lost connections. The impurities of my affection for roles and recognition had to be burned off. While it felt like more loss than my heart could handle, a change within was my big win. Church was not the problem; I had a heart issue.

It is almost automatic to feel the absence of God in hard times. Because I elevated my roles above my relationship with him, duty replaced my delight, and my faith had grown stale. Refining was a gift of grace I did not know I needed. It is counter-intuitive to think of loss as gain, but that is exactly what I learned in that season. While I generally avoid hard things or expend too much energy finding someone to blame, I learned to stay the course, endure the fire, and trust the process. Difficult things don't have to be destructive. Some of our best lessons include the unlearning of unhealthy habits and patterns.

My season of refining tarried for four exhausting years. Enduring the season was not without challenges. I often felt my spirit would be crushed before I experienced healing or relief. I am prone to flee, so enduring the messy middle was a critical lesson I learned on my field trip through pain. While I am not yet fully transformed in believing my worth is not tied to work, I am different. I am not saying "yes" to every opportunity that presents itself. I am exercising the muscle of believing who I am is good—not because of what I have done or will do, but because I am made in the image of God. Sometimes transformation is quick, but other times it is a long game. *Who told you that?* is a phrase I regularly apply to discern where my feet are planted because I unconsciously return to my old rhythms. Taking a minute to reflect is a simple way to course correct and get back on track.

Is there something you have been holding onto that you no longer need? Are you avoiding the refining fire and missing the opportunity to mature in a specific area of your life? We get to our strength by enduring the fiery trials of life. When the temperature gets hotter than we think we can endure, we can trust that we are in the process of transformation.

Endure the fire. Avoid the blame game. Surrender yourself to the process. Ask yourself where the trial is rooted. Let go of the old ways that no longer fit in this season. Be open to unlearning old patterns to create a lasting change deep within you. Consider God's heart of love for you.

I know learning how to unlearn might be painful, but in just a little while, you will emerge as pure as gold and as strong as stone. Start small. Build one habit at a time. Avoid aiming for perfection. Lean into incremental change. Commit to starting. Transformation is always worth the investment.

REFLECTION: Are you facing a trial in your life? Is there something you need to unlearn to make room for something new? How have you experienced the transformation process in your life?

GOING DEEPER: Read Romans 5:3-5. What does this passage teach you about suffering? Are you inclined to avoid suffering or assume it is unnecessary? How do these verses reframe your understanding of the good that comes from life's trials?

Chapter Ten

Catch and Release

* We are wise to listen as much as we speak—if not more.

Every day may not be good…but there's
something good in every day.
–Alice Morse Earle

FISHING IS NOT MY THING. Slimy and sharp
textures are better left to someone else. Not only that,
if I am going to sit and wait for anything, it better
come with queso. In South Texas, we have lakes and
the ocean in our backyard, so fishing as a sport and
hobby is very much a thing. We have Bass fishing
clubs at our schools, and the kids are good fishermen
because their practice matches their passion. They
spend hours waiting for a bite—only to unhook the
fish, release it back into the water, and start all over
again. And some call this fun.

A few summers ago, we took a trip to the coast
before our two oldest returned to college. The guys
were heading out early to do some deep-sea fishing,
so my daughter and I set up at the pool to enjoy the
day. Did I mention that both boys struggle with

motion-sickness? One of the boys rides the struggle bus hard, and the other one can usually sleep to curb the impact. Both were out on the water. The excursion was not a catch and release trip, though, and the more people on the boat, the more fish in the haul. For serious fishermen, you do not head home until you've reached your limit. That may have been a good tip to share with my boys prior to their departure. Hours later, they returned with a lot of fish and even more stories of sea sickness misery.

● ● ●

The more I think about it—fishing is a lot like parenting. That just felt like a massive stretch for some of you—I know. Let me explain. When I was in high school, I thought I knew everything. I kept my sights on my 18th birthday because adulthood would welcome a new level of freedom. Just typing that out makes me giggle. Oh, how wrong I was. Society talks about the legality of adulthood, but anyone over 18 knows the necessity of guidance and a firm foundation under your feet before taking off into the great unknown. Now that my last one is inching closer to legal adulthood, I realize how much 18-years-old feels more like 18-months-old and less like an adult. That is not a criticism of him; he is a great kid, but there is so much left to experience. Parenting is about giving and giving and giving. It includes so much practicing and waiting. Some parents teach a lesson and send their kids back out to put it into practice. Others use parenting to their benefit instead of for the benefit of the child.

With a *fishing for food* parenting mindset, when the limit is reached, the work is done. That 18th birthday becomes a rite of passage — while parents tout the joys of their new freedom. In all my years of living, I have never stopped wanting my parents to parent me. They have the wisdom of the years on their side, and I do not dare think I have an advantage over them. Why would we believe parenting ends at a certain age? My theory is that we get tired because the pressure of parenting on top of everything else is a lot. We long for someone else to take a turn.

A *catch and release* parenting mindset involves a lot of waiting and repetition. Launching children into the world is done with intentionality and expectation. Like the fisherman waiting to see what will happen, parents instruct, send out, and reel it in when necessary. Teach and guide, send out, return, untangle the line, teach again, repair the line, and release. They expect to repeat the process again and again. The 18th birthday milestone is not seen as the end but as a time to adjust to a long-cast strategy.

● ● ●

Intentionality is one of my core values. Being aware and purposeful feels a lot like love to me. Because I have struggled with feeling unseen, it is a sincere desire of my heart to be sure those around me feel seen and known. It is much easier to live in the comfort of our own little bubbles and be consumed and concerned about little more than that, but you cannot be intentional and self-absorbed at the same time. When my parenting time was reduced to a little more than half with my two older children, a new urgency was born in me. Sharing custody required me to use instructional moments purposefully. We talked about everything. We played. We memorized scripture. We worked to create a family identity that was clear and where everyone had a place.

While learning a new normal, I dedicated myself to being as intentional as possible in my parenting. The kids could tell you stories about the times I blew it. Many times my parenting fishing line got tangled up, and we had to cut it and start all over. There were times I let my own desires overshadow their need to be small, and I yelled when I would have rather listened. Even so, I was committed to getting up another day and trying again. I had to make room for my mistakes instead of beating myself up repeatedly. This practice continues today.

● ● ●

When my oldest was a senior in high school, I had the idea to meet him for lunch once a week. I hoped he would want to, and we could use the time to grow our relationship before he left the house. My parenting, in many ways, was just beginning to ramp up. The weight of all the things I had not taught him woke me up in the middle of the night. Did he know to wash his hands after touching raw meat? Had I prepared him for the long nights of loneliness living away from all that was familiar? Was he scared or nervous about going away? Carving out time to sit together, talk, and listen was the best gift we gave each other in that season. Specifically, listening was the part he needed from me. I brought lots of questions to our weekly lunch dates, but I paid attention to his needs and backed off when he was *done*.

We do a lot of talking in parenting. We do too much talking in parenting. There is a time for that, but it seems we forget to release by asking questions and listening to responses. We forget that our little sponges grow into young adults with their own thoughts and ideas. When we keep talking, they eventually stop talking and even listening.

Senior lunches with the oldest parlayed into similar dates when my daughter was a senior. Those were some of the sweetest times in our relationship. We talked about all manner of things and began to understand each other beyond the parent-child relationship.

Intentional listening begets a deeper connection and relationship.

I am no expert in parenting. One secret weapon I discovered is asking questions and listening with intention. That decision translates into presence. Being aware invites depth and trust in relationships and is the essence of catch-and-release parenting. Draw in, inspect, and then send the little fish off to explore the big world. We cannot know when to reel it in, so to speak, if our hands don't remain on the rod. This is not a call to control; it is the awareness that proximity is necessary. In parenting, the job is never really done; the job description just changes.

Now that our two oldest have added others into our family through marriage, I see the gift of the parenting long-game. Way before they married, I committed myself to loving whomever they loved. That decision meant asking lots of questions, remembering important details, and creating a welcoming space. I have watched countless mothers cling to their sons and ice out anyone their sons love. I was on the receiving end of that in my first marriage, and I vowed never to do that to my children. Cultivating relationships is a lot of work that is not necessarily easy or immediately fruitful. However, when we move with intentionality, we measure every word and stay dialed in to the needs of our children.

The people in my family are my favorites. I wonder if that would be the case if I had just thrown them into the world with well-wishes on their 18th birthday. So many things pull at our attention and fight for our affection in this life. We get to decide how we will respond and what gets priority. No matter where you are in this equation—a parent of young children, a young adult desiring a deeper relationship with a parent, a parent of adult children, or loving children who are not your own, there is still hope in your relationship. Maybe everything won't be good, but you can find something good in everything.

Resolve to be intentional as you move throughout your relationships. Be present, ask good questions, and listen for the answers, but don't forget to give yourself the same level of grace. We often tend to others and neglect the next steps forward in our own lives. Intentionality means we are deliberate and purposeful in the questions we ask ourselves, the time we invest in listening to ourselves, and the decisions that flow from that posture. That is not necessarily easy, but we can learn a lot from healthy people around us. We are wise to listen as much as we speak—if not more.

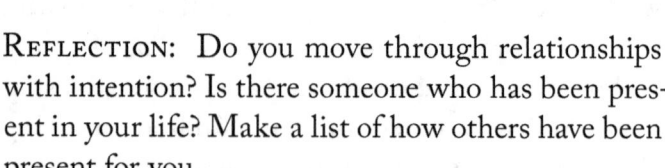

REFLECTION: Do you move through relationships with intention? Is there someone who has been present in your life? Make a list of how others have been present for you.

GOING DEEPER: Read Philippians 2:3 and 1 Peter 4:8. What is the central theme in both verses? How can that guide your relationships? What might that look like practically?

Chapter Eleven

Moving Forward

* If something no longer fits, we have permission to let it go. We cannot lay hold of something new when we have not let go of the past.

What you aren't changing, you're choosing.
—Nicki Koziarz

EVERY EXPERIENCE IN LIFE offers a lesson we can ignore or collect. We get to choose if the twists and turns take us out or teach us. Some lessons will give us enough to get through a moment, and some will not fully stick until we enter later seasons. When I lost a good friend in a tragic car accident, I learned the value of saying all the things that matter when you have the opportunity. Much later, I understood the seed of reconciliation that was planted amidst the tragedy. While hurt often happens in the context of relationships, we also find healing in the context of community.

When we refuse to take an honest look at our lives, we miss opportunities to heal, walk in wholeness, and see beauty rising from the rubble. It took me many years to be ready to face the long line of devastation in the wake of my life experiences, decisions, and trauma. I missed growth opportunities because the full weight of my story was too much to face. Until I was ready, I lived in fear. Mind you, it took a long time for me to realize fear had stunted my growth. Let me assure you, I was not moving forward; I was numb and side-stepping through life. My moves were dutiful but not full of joy or hope.

As my healing journey continues, I am listening, watching, and waiting for the lessons that will lead me to the next mile marker. For a girl who learned to silence her needs and soldier on, this means slowing down and staying in the uncomfortable moments. It was at a particularly pressed moment when a phrase downloaded into my mind. *What you don't grieve becomes a grievance.* The list of my grievances centered around voicelessness, so I spent some time thinking about what I had not grieved that may have led me to that space. The pondering caused me to consider my relationship with grieving.

The grief file folder in my mind was empty except for one word. Crying. I rarely cried. Survivors cannot bother with pausing to cry or feel; it is too dangerous to let down their guard. Feelings poke holes in the armor intended to provide protection, but what keeps something from coming in, also keeps things from coming out. If you silence feelings of sadness, you also miss moments of joy. How to grieve was not a lesson I ever remember learning.

Grief is more than tears. I know that now. Grief is an acknowledgment of desires and losses. Grief requires time and attention. Grief invites honest reflection and admission. Grief includes inward and outward expressions. Synonyms of grief are heartbreak, anguish, sorrow, suffering, and distress. Grief hits in unspeakable places of the soul. I picture grief as a thick fog impacting visibility. It can be disorienting and debilitating. No wonder I avoided it for so long, but the truth is—living with a long list of grievances has the same effect. Not only do grievances make others uncomfortable, but they are often unsolvable because they are focused on the wrong audience. Grievances are outwardly focused, while grief is an inward journey.

● ● ●

When the phrase *what you don't grieve becomes a grievance* landed on me, I had to ask God to reveal what I had avoided grieving. Grievances often precede us and impact our personalities. I immediately knew my primary grievance, and if we have ever shared a cup of tea, you know it too. The thing I talk about ad nauseam is the value of a woman's voice and the opportunities to use her gifts and talents. This lands particularly rough for me in church settings where I have experienced quite the opposite of a warm welcome. The result of feeling unwanted is a deeply held sense of resentment toward men in leadership. My experience with feeling voiceless as a woman in church leadership was real, but it had become a grievance. As I pondered the grievance, I began digging to see if I could find what was under it. What had I avoided grieving? I did not have to wait long before the answer hit me.

My childhood was hard. My parent's tumultuous relationship instilled a deep fear and sense of loss in me. In the wake of their divorce, my sense of self was compromised. This is where I pinpoint my failure to grieve. At ten-years-old, I moved toward silencing my needs and compromising my voice. While I longed to be affirmed and valued, I felt quite the opposite. This was linked to my perception of the storm and my interpretation of the actions of my parents. Inarticulate loneliness moved in and became an odd comfort and companion. I had to grieve the things I needed but did not receive as a little girl. While I had accepted the snippets of love and care I had been given and found a way to move on, I had not grieved the unmet longings.

Moving on is not the same as moving forward. Moving on requires a decision and knowledge; moving forward requires surrender and healing. Which one feels easier? Which one makes space for grieving? The answers to those questions are obvious, but what makes us freeze from moving forward is that moving on is a culturally acceptable choice. We celebrate the strength of others without examining the condition of their climb to get to the appearance of said strength.

• • •

Every field trip in elementary school involved visiting Abe Lincoln's Springfield home, his tomb, or New Salem—where he floated in on the Sangamon River and lived during his twenties. By the time I was ten, I could have made a living giving tours at any one of the sites. I am kidding, but only sort of. My favorite trip was always Lincoln's tomb—a humble monument located in a large cemetery with ordinary people. An estimated 200,000 people venture to the tomb each year, and I was happy to be a number among many. The mausoleum fascinated me. Standing in the burial room felt somber and surreal, but there was something that also scared me a little. Was Abe really in that enclosure? Was there any chance he would emerge?

A monument commemorates a person or event. It serves as a mile-marker of sorts. When visiting a monument, we are invited to remember. While I continue to be intrigued by Lincoln's tomb, I have also grown increasingly aware of the danger of making monuments out of moments in our lives. The good and bad moments of our lives are not the full story. They make up moments along the journey, but there is a great temptation to erect a monument around one and miss opportunities to continue moving forward. Without realizing it, this is what I had done with feeling voiceless. Because I did not grieve, I inadvertently built a monument for my grievances.

Do you know what else happens at a monument? We invite visitors, we hire employees, we sell merchandise, we give tours, and we tell the story again and again. The hurt I experienced became a monument when it should have just been a moment in my life, pointing me to the next one. Grievances lined the walls and told the story of my unresolved wounds. Who wants to visit that? Moving forward requires intentionality. We get to remember the story without getting stuck in the plot.

How do you know if you have made a monument out of a moment? Do you feel like a broken record? Have you elevated a moment or experience to the point you have stopped imagining anything better or different? Can you imagine the next step on the journey? Is there room in your life for another perspective? Are you carrying the weight of the world over one misstep? Has a wound taken center-stage? Is your energy centered around what *you* need to do? If so, you may have constructed a monument. Maybe your body is inviting you to remember the story and grieve in that space.

When people visit Lincoln's tomb, they are inclined to think of his contributions to society. The monument is a place of honor for a lifetime of service, not a single moment in his life. What would happen if we approached our lives with the same mindset? The sum of our life experiences contributes to the greater story that leads us forward if we are vigilant to watch, wait, and trust the process. Getting stuck on a moment impedes the next one, but the collection of our moments provides opportunities to grow in wisdom.

● ● ●

Letting go is one of the hardest two-word initiatives. My instinct is to white-knuckle my way through life. I like order and control, and if we can throw in a good dose of reason, I am one happy camper. My friend Karen said she has clothes for three people in her closet, the sizes she had once worn, the size she is currently wearing, and the size she hopes to wear again. We laughed at her explanation at the moment, but the imagery stuck with me. I can relate to holding on to things that no longer fit.

Carrying something ill-fitting into a new season becomes an obstacle for moving forward. I am in a season of life where my body is changing. A menopause midsection that will stand for nothing less than making a statement has emerged, and while I cannot be sure, I think my hips have started expanding their territory too. Ignoring this was my first response-obviously-but as the pile of pants I could no longer button grew, it became impossible to look the other way. Like Karen, I could not and did not get rid of them, and they taunted me every time I entered my closet. I was stuck in what I once was, and I painfully poured myself into tight jeans that hugged all the wrong places—stretching the zipper to the maximum capacity.

When the pain got too great, I decided to act. I loaded myself up, drove to a local discount store, and hit the sale rack, determined to find a pair of jeans in a size that felt comfortable. Trying them on confirmed what my midsection had been begging me to understand. The pants piled up in my closet no longer fit.

How tempting it is to carry something old into a new season. To shove the friendship from last season into the current season. To squeeze the answer from one circumstance into the next one. When we do this, we forget to make room for something new and space for something completely different. If something no longer fits, we have permission to let it go. We cannot lay hold of something new when we have not let go of the past.

Letting go does not involve ignoring; it involves acknowledgment and believing that the story is still in progress. Trust is a critical component in letting go to move forward. In her book, *Flooded: The Five Best Decisions to Make When Life is Hard and Doubt is Rising*, Nicki Koziarz reminds readers that what they aren't changing, they are choosing.[9] Let that thought linger for a second. We often blame others and point fingers, but the onus is on us. We can make decisions that change the story or sit in the saga. I am guilty of wanting my midsection situation to change but doing nothing to make that happen. Letting go involves choosing something different.

The way forward is to marry surrender and trust. Letting go of what no longer fits, grieving what hurts, and walking through moments requires much. Not wanting to invest the energy to do the work is what pushes most of us to erect monuments and settle for good enough. I don't know what keeps you from putting in the effort, but I know the essence of my stubbornness. Fear of failure. Fear of disappointment. Doubt. Unbelief. I see the thread that runs from what I did not grieve to this space.

When I am afraid, I forget God. When I am filled with doubt, my attention is fixed on what I can or cannot do. I am learning to believe two attributes of God: he is loving and attentive. Those are things I deeply desired as a child. If I let my childhood experiences dictate the journey, I move on—not forward. If I allow the character of God to guide my path, the pressure to get it right no longer rests on my shoulders, and I can take a step forward, surrendering my inclination to prove my worth and trust his love.

It is not up to me. Friend, it is not up to you either. Release the tight grip that has prevented you from grabbing the wisdom in front of you. The way forward includes clearly understanding what work is ours and what we need to surrender. Letting go isn't a step backward; it is a step forward.

REFLECTION: Is there something you hoped would change, but hasn't? Can you ponder the step you can take in moving forward? How does your healing impact those closest to you?

GOING DEEPER: Read Isaiah 43:19. Do you believe this is possible in your life? What step do you feel compelled to take today? Will you?

SECTION THREE

Propagating Hope

Chapter Twelve

Choosing Kindness over Convenience

* People aren't problems. They are the point.

Kindness is love with flesh and a face.
–Alyssa De Los Santos

MY INSTINCT IS TO PROTECT MY INTERESTS.
I have a proclivity toward proving my value through endless cycles of work. My solution for any problem is to work harder, which may be the most exhausting trait I embody. Because of my nature, generosity is not my native language, but I have discovered a way to strengthen what is not instinctive. Choosing kindness when it is inconvenient loosens the grip of my self-centeredness.

We are faced with choices moment by moment. How we respond to traffic, interact with others, look at people with different political views, and posture ourselves toward those in need reveals what we value. We might be kind. We might be rude. We might not even take the time to see beyond ourselves. No matter what, we have choices about how we engage with others. I have built my adult life around the concept of showing up and seeing others, and I am deeply devoted to the call to be kind, and yet I still fail when I have forgotten that being kind means welcoming strangers.

● ● ●

In the throes of a harried morning, I raced into the lab, hoping to have my blood drawn quickly. As is a sign of the times, every patient checks in using an electronic device. To my absolute delight, the waiting room was nearly empty, with only one person checking in ahead of me that morning. Things appeared to be conveniently leaning in my favor.

The older woman in front of me spent an inordinate amount of time fumbling through the check-in process. The commentary in my head was just south of kind. I declared that she only needed to enter her phone number to reach the next screen, yet she kept returning to the home screen. My silent frustration grew to a near-audible intolerance in the form of sighing; I wanted to sign in, get my labs drawn, and get on with the rest of my day. This slowdown was unwelcome and was completely disrupting my plan for the day.

Though the slowdown of an interruption is typically inconvenient, it's generally fertile soil for learning a necessary life lesson. While the older woman struggled to enter her information using the electronic system, I struggled to see her immediate need. After several failed attempts, she turned to me and muttered something about her frustration before stepping aside. Smiling politely, I stepped toward the device and away from the inconvenience. My pride swelled as I quickly and successfully signed in on my first attempt. I had shown her.

Puffed up, I took a vacant seat and waited my turn. As quickly as I turned away from the flustered woman, a conviction grew in my spirit about a missed opportunity to be kind and meet a tangible need. My selfishness made it easy to be unaware of others. The interruption of the woman's struggle, although initially causing a wave of arrogant pride, invited me to look beyond my own little world and reconsider my attitude.

With the weight of shame heavy on me, I looked at the woman through new eyes. She was visibly shaken. My heart melted as I took in the depth of her despair. I no longer saw an interruption sitting across from me in the waiting room; I saw a woman in need. As our eyes locked, she told me she felt dizzy. Without thinking, I moved to the chair next to her and reached over to hold her hand. Her voice trembled as she took my hand and told me her story. Tears pooled in my eyes, and I assured her I would help. That is when she revealed she couldn't remember her telephone number. The previous moments flashed through my mind, and it occurred to me what was happening during the minutes before this one.

Every time she arrived at the screen requesting her number, she panicked and returned to the home screen. Again and again, she found herself staring at the screen, reminding her what she had forgotten. Her interruption became mine. *What she couldn't remember, I could not afford to forget.* She was a person with an authentic need, and I had the time and ability to invest. When an employee surfaced, I asked if they could put her in line using the orders she held in her hands. I did not mention that she could not remember her phone number, but I wonder if they instinctively knew.

Since she had stepped aside to let me sign in, I was called back before she was. As the phlebotomist worked to draw my blood, I absorbed a valuable lesson I could have missed that morning. Interruptions are opportunities to be open to exercising kindness. While it is easy to hyper-focus on the inconvenience of a slowdown, a lesson of wisdom is usually waiting to be learned.

The woman struggling to remember her telephone number was someone's daughter, sister, aunt, wife, mother, grandmother, and friend. The interruption was an opportunity to stand in the gap for her loved ones by choosing the ministry of kindness. That is exactly what I would want for my parents, sisters, husband, children, family, and friends. I can't say I am great at accepting the slowdown of interruptions, but I am learning to see the opportunity wrapped in inconvenience.

Pride forfeits involvement, but it is entirely possible that the point of an interruption is to see others. People aren't problems. They are the point. What she couldn't remember became fertile ground for what I couldn't afford to forget. We are inextricably connected in community. We were given the gift of relationship for shouldering burdens, building one another up, and cheering for each other.

Choosing kindness will not always prove profitable or even comfortable.

● ● ●

My mom walked through a season of depression that threatened to take her life. So many hours were invested in discussing plans that might turn the tide on her mental and physical health. Our fear for her was palpable. In a last-ditch effort, I booked a flight home to accompany her to a doctor's appointment. While waiting for a connecting flight, I found myself thinking about what I might say to the doctor that would not further injure my mother. Everything felt heavy.

Once I boarded the flight and found my seat, silently rejoicing that the middle seat was unoccupied, I settled in for the final leg of my trip. I anticipated rehearsing what I wanted to say to my mom and her doctor, but it quickly became apparent that my well-planned quiet time would have to wait. Though there was an empty seat next to me, the person occupying the aisle seat asked one question that led to another that led to a conversation.

He shared about his surgery and follow-up appointment, requiring a flight to the area. When he asked me about the reason for my travel, I saw kindness in his eyes as I told the truth about my mom. He listened attentively and asked meaningful questions. I had made things uncomfortable for us both, but he made space for the story without trying to pretty it up or fix it. Compassion is the litmus test of vulnerability.

I was shocked when the flight attendants announced we would be landing shortly. The time had passed quickly because of the lengthy conversation with a perfect stranger. As we deplaned, my new friend turned to me and said he hoped things with my mom turned out better than I expected. His words gave me the strength to step off the plane and into the raging storm of my mother's illness, and things eventually turned around for her.

Kindness is not necessarily convenient. It will, no doubt, include interruptions, uncomfortable moments, and missteps. It might mess up your entire calendar, but it will never allow you to stay in a place of self-centeredness. Kindness looks to the needs of others. It is a perspective adjuster. It reorders our priorities. Though we tend to think of them as unwelcome, interruptions are opportunities to be open to exercising kindness.

Kindness is not a trend to get behind; it is a daily decision to put someone else's needs above our own. It is the act of welcoming strangers and inconveniences. It is choosing to see people as individual stories walking around to enhance ours. Kindness shows up and offers a way out; it does not wait for an invitation; it barges right in and does the dishes or pours you a glass of your favorite drink. It takes on many forms to reach into the crevices of our souls.

● ● ●

The day I had my labs drawn, fear in the older woman's eyes invited me to be sacrificial. As my appointment finished her name was called, so I leaned toward her to say I would remain in the waiting room until she finished. When she finished, I offered to walk her to her car and sincerely hoped she was not driving. To my delight, her husband was waiting in the parking lot. I retrieved the smile I had forgotten to use when I initially met his wife and let him know she was not feeling well. Kindness told me to bite my tongue about reporting the forgotten phone number because he probably already knew. Maybe my decision to be present for her was less about her and more about him. But perhaps it was all about me learning to get comfortably uncomfortable outside myself.

Tears spilled from my eyes as I walked to my car. I had not anticipated learning a life lesson that morning, but I intended to pocket something I hope never to forget. People are the point. Interruptions are opportunities. Kindness is always in style. We have choices. We are strangers someone else might be inconvenienced by. Let's not too soon forget we are not always the hero; we, too, find ourselves frustrated, confused, and reaching for the kindness of another.

Choosing kindness is always the best choice. We get to extend what we hope others will extend to us. Welcome the inconveniences of today as opportunities to learn valuable lessons, to be kind in ways that impact all your tomorrows, and to grow in wisdom.

REFLECTION: Are you inclined to see interruptions as problems or opportunities? Think of a time when someone extended kindness to you. How did that experience shape you? What choice can you make today to start exercising your right to be kind?

GOING DEEPER: Read Proverbs 16:24 and Proverbs 12:25. What is the value of kindness? Have you accepted the kindness of God so that you can extend kindness toward others?

Chapter Thirteen

The Ministry of Presence

* Presence is a powerful thing. When we offer ourselves and what we have to others, connection becomes a healing balm for the soul.

No matter where you go, there you are.
—Mary Engelbreit

IT WASN'T REALLY WHAT HE WAS DOING that
caused the breath to catch in my throat, just the fact
that he was there. While I knew there was power
in presence, it had never been so palpable as when I
pulled in the driveway and saw him mowing my lawn.
I had not asked; he had shown up on his own accord.

As a newly single mother, I was reconstructing
my daily life. I was worried about my children, so I
busied myself establishing a new family identity. We
were going to be okay in time, and confident stability
was one of the only things I could offer my children
as their normal was turned upside down by divorce.
How I would squeeze in mowing the lawn and tending to the needs of the house had not even crossed
my mind. I had no plan for daily duties. When a

house is on fire, you focus on getting your people out safely—everything else pales in significance. That was where I was.

I had taken the children to a movie to escape the constant reminders of his absence. It was money I did not have to spend, but it was a decision I couldn't afford to miss. We reached the top of the incline on our road when I spotted his car. He didn't ask to come over; he just did what he knew we needed. The presence of a church elder mowing my lawn caused a flood of tears to pour out from the deep place of my soul that was longing to be held and protected.

Presence is a powerful thing. When we offer ourselves and what we have to others, connection becomes a healing balm for the soul. When we withhold ourselves from others, emotional loneliness takes a toll. The ministry of presence is when we choose to show up for someone without being asked. It is perceiving a need and deciding we are part of the answer. It is running in when others are running out. It is holding a hand and silencing unnecessary words.

It was just a lawn being mowed at that moment, but it was also a step toward restoration and trust. People could be counted on. I was not too much, and my needs were not too great. Life would be different; our wounds would heal. One day we would focus less on the absence and more on the value of presence.

Through the presence of absence, I was invited to deal with my pain. The palpable pain of my children, the innocent bystanders, ushered me from the momentary suffering to the old familiar territory of being a child of divorce myself. When the kids were with me, I would do everything I could to create a routine full of hope, but on the weekends they were with their father, I struggled to get off the couch. Without their presence, it wasn't easy to find purpose and joy.

● ● ●

The transition from one house to the other was nearly unbearable for all of us. My daughter would cry on Sunday nights after settling back in after a weekend visit with her dad. Although completely wiped out from the weekend, sleep would elude her as heartache overwhelmed her. The pattern became predictable. I would tuck her in and slowly back away from her room, hoping to avoid what I knew would follow and praying for a break in the pattern.

"Mommy, I need you." Her tiny voice would drift from her room.

Heavy-hearted and still just outside her door, I always responded to the plea by reentering her room, sitting down on the edge of the bed, and asking about her weekend. The story rarely changed, a typical weekend filled with adventures, hugs, and surprises. I listened while a smile masked my pain and lingered until it seemed okay to close the day with a gentle prayer. It was always then that the longing for her father's presence overwhelmed her tiny heart.

"Can I call daddy to make sure he is okay? Mommy, I miss him so much."

"I know baby," was always the response that escaped my lips. It was all I had to offer.

I realized his absence was the focus of both our hearts. Though not spoken, my girl's baby blue eyes, welled up with tears, revealed the concerns of her heart: anxiety that the next visit wouldn't come, fear that one day his love might run dry, and sadness that another night would end with her in a home without him.

I would kiss her forehead, brush away her golden locks, and watch the tempest rise. No books are written specifically for the inaudible language of a heart ripping in two, yet you always know when you have heard it.

"I just want daddy."

Fighting the talons of temptation, I swallowed a litany of selfish responses, scooped her into my arms, and quietly recalled my deep longing to be loved and protected and valued and delighted in. My heart grew heavier as I acknowledged the void in both of us that would always be part of our stories.

Attempting to navigate the waves of a plethora of emotions, I would embrace her tiny frame with the reassurance of my presence and love. With that touch, the tears dropped, and the all-too-familiar storm raged again. As she wept, I cried with her and for her. Mustering all my strength, I cradled her in my arms to console her.

"I love you, baby girl," I whispered as I laid her back in bed.

"God please take her pain away," I inaudibly pleaded as I calculated the many storms to come in the wake of his absence.

For years this story played out like a scene from Groundhog Day, and one day it hit me. Instead of fussing about what absence had created, I could leverage the power of presence. That was what I had been doing all along. He was no longer in our home, but I was. The ministry of presence was about showing up fully and holding her as the storm waged, comforting her when anxiety called, and listening as she shared her longings. I got to be the one to hold her broken pieces until she was ready to put them back together. She trusted me to keep her safe.

● ● ●

Throughout my life, I often deferred my attention to the palpable pain of absence, which only led to feeling powerless and stuck. The ministry of presence started healing my broken heart and strengthening me for the rest of the journey. It opened my eyes to the various ways the power of presence intersected authentic need. Presence is like a watering station on a journey through the desert. When the soul is dehydrated, it provides nutrients to continue the trek.

During another particularly painful season of my life, presence was the key that turned the tide. Sadness about a family situation had added undue pressure on my marriage. You know how stress has a way of blowing everything up, right? That is where I was. In addition to heartbreak, I was also feeling lonely. In a moment of vulnerability, I texted two of my friends who are more like sisters. It was my SOS because I was fighting a battle with feelings and losing.

A question on the text thread stands out to me. One of the sisters asked if I needed them. I responded with one word—maybe—and put my phone down to get in the shower. Shortly after finishing, there was a slight knock on the bathroom door. My husband told me that my two friends were there and asked me if I wanted him to send them in. While I would have preferred to have all the problems disappear, I opted to accept the gift of their presence. The towel was still on my head, and my threadbare robe was my wardrobe, but as soon as they walked in, I fell into their arms. They didn't ask a million questions. They just held me, and it was everything I didn't know I needed at that moment.

The ministry of presence might be mowing a lawn, delivering a meal, making a phone call, sending a letter, asking a question, paying someone's overdue electric bill, stopping to help change a tire, or offering a sincere prayer. It might be saying *I am here with you* by showing up without having to be asked. It's driving across town to watch your friend's child in a theater performance. It is allowing yourself to be inconvenienced for the sake of someone else. It's getting on the floor, sitting in silence, and offering a tissue. It's remembering the painful anniversary of the death of a loved one. It is sacrificing and choosing to be a "yes" in a world of "no".

Choosing presence might cost you a lot, but it could be our most significant investment. When we focus on how we have been wronged or abandoned, we become consumed with the hole left by absence, but when we shift our focus to showing up for others, we remember the gift of connection and the power of presence.

● ● ●

Corrie ten Boom demonstrated the power of presence in a story she told about seeing a guard from the concentration camp where she was imprisoned in the crowd while she delivered a talk on forgiveness. Although her experience at Ravensbrück was insufferable, she focused less on what she lost and more on what she gained. Following her speech, the guard approached her. She remembered him, but she was sure he didn't recognize her. He asked for her forgiveness. It was a blanket request as he had come to know God and needed freedom from the heavy burden of the memory of pain he inflicted on others.[10]

Corrie had a choice at that moment. Who would have blamed her for denying forgiveness? Do you know what she did? She recognized the ministry of presence, and she extended forgiveness. While he probably could not recall the injury he inflicted specifically on her, don't you know she understood the prison he had lived in over the years. She had the key to free him; it was the shape of her presence.

Corrie's decision to stay present in the moment with the guard is a reminder that our perspective helps heal our soul. Bitterness and resentment would have been reasonable responses to his request, but she understood that those would keep her trapped in a prison of pain. Her forgiveness freed him, but it also released her. She had a choice.

● ● ●

My little girl who used to cry on Sunday nights became a young lady who moved one thousand miles away. When she opted to attend college in my home state, my only relief was knowing family was a short drive away. The tricky thing for me was that I had to learn to value the presence of others. There were dive meets I could not attend and banquets I missed, but something beautiful was born in the place of my absence.

My family filled the gap that the miles created. One sister took on the mantle of being my girl's stand-in mom. Yes, she was her aunt, but she approached needs as a mother would. She sent me videos of dives I couldn't witness in person. She cleaned apartments that were not quite ready for move-in (thank you college apartment companies). My other sister would stop by my girl's place whenever she passed through town. They shared meaningful conversations born in deep love. Most of the miles added to my parent's odometer are a direct result of driving my girl from school to the airport and vice versa.

My family showed up when I could not. They elevated the power of presence. They made choices that fleshed out love. They had plenty on their calendars but carved out time for my girl. They used the ministry of presence to quiet my fears, comfort her heart, and stand in the gap. Her success in college is a direct result of my people's choices to sacrifice and show up.

Presence also looked like a cul-de-sac of neighbors hauling items out of my garage when a Texas freeze saw fit to introduce us to the joy of a busted water pipe. Before I could get the word out, help came running in with hands and tools ready to work. Friends descended and greeted one another as if they were arriving at a summer barbeque instead of schlepping through the flood in our garage. Bags of groceries that did not require water to prepare or clean up were deposited on our kitchen island. Showing up and contributing what you have for the common good is how the power of presence takes a stressful moment and makes it an unforgettable adventure.

These are a few examples of how presence has powerfully intersected seasons of my life. Can you recall a specific time when presence healed your hurt or lessened the pain of the blow? As it turns out, we are the answer to the problem of pain and absence. We get to choose our response in the middle of suffering and joy. While it might be inconvenient to show up, it will also be incomparable. "I am with you" are words that just might save a life.

We won't always get it right, but we can celebrate the opportunity to use our presence as a tool of positive persuasion and power. If you are ever given the option to focus on presence or absence, choose presence. When we pivot from a perspective focused on loss to one focused on gain, everyone wins. Tuck this wisdom away for a rainy day. The ministry of presence might change someone's life forever, and it just might be yours.

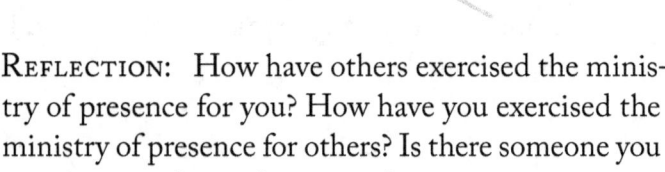

REFLECTION: How have others exercised the ministry of presence for you? How have you exercised the ministry of presence for others? Is there someone you can show up for in this season?

GOING DEEPER: Read Luke 5:17-20. What is the ministry of presence in this passage? What is the result of the friend's decision to remain present in the story? How does this encourage you in your relationships?

Chapter Fourteen

Tell the Story

* Don't look the other way and hope for
  the best...

*There is no greater agony than bearing an
untold story inside you.*
—*Maya Angelou*

SEVERAL YEARS AGO, WE HAD TO EVACUATE
our home. In the thick of a significant drought, with
grass resembling hay and crunching underfoot like
fall leaves, our area was desperate for rain. Small grass
fires had started and been extinguished in our area,
so when I saw the smoke rising, I knew immediately
imminent danger was unfolding.

It started as a small line of smoke rising over the
rooflines of homes in my neighborhood. What began
as a hint of a distant fire grew quickly into visible
flames. Standing on my front lawn, I was growing
concerned for our safety. Intuition is an excellent
guide in emergencies, and I decided to follow mine
by packing an overnight bag and driving away from
the threat and toward safety.

Not long after we pulled away from our neighborhood, a mandatory evacuation was issued. The fire, which had grown wild, was predicted to jump the farm road that separated us. In a dry season, a tiny spark can cause enough flame to manifest into great devastation.

I will always remember driving back to our neighborhood early the next morning. While I was grateful our home avoided a direct hit, acres ravaged by fire stretched for miles. The land was still smoldering, and a thick cloud of ominous smoke hung in the air declaring danger was still lurking. The images around us silenced idle conversation. A tiny spark had caused a wildfire.

Driving down the same stretch of road today, I cannot help but notice the lasting effects of the fire that raged several years ago. Because the land was not cleared after the fire, dead trees occupy the space where they were once full of life. They serve as a reminder that a fire ravaged the area. In the years that have followed, new life has grown around the dead trees.

My mind entertained the image of the lifeless trees in the center of the new growth. I am inclined to "clear the land" after a devastating experience or interaction. I tend to uproot and remove any evidence of tragedy, but here is the thing, the dead trees that stand on those acres tell a story. A fire tore through the land. The new life growing up around the trees tells a story, too. Growth and new life happen even amid tragedy and death.

When we walk through the fire, the story does not automatically end with destruction and death. If we give it time, something new can grow around that hard memory. The dead trees on that stretch of land speak of a time when fire snuffed out life, but the life around the dead trees speaks of the power of endurance and resilience.

We tend to cover up our scars and hide our pain. Scars get a bum rap in our beauty-obsessed culture. There are countless remedies to reduce the visibility of scars, underscoring how we are told to feel about them, but scars are not ugly. Scars are storylines. They imply past wounding and serve as evidence of healing.

I have the tiniest scar on one of my heels. It is dainty and almost undetectable at first glance. Sometimes I run my finger over it to remind me that a problematic beginning did not disrupt the moments, days, and years that followed.

My scar tells a story of the significant case of jaundice I had at birth that was dangerous enough to land me an extended stay in the hospital after my mother was released. When a blood sample is taken from a newborn, they prick the heel. So, my little heel was repeatedly pricked to check bilirubin levels, an IV drip adorned my tiny head, and my storyline began.

The scar on my heel serves as a reminder of the provision of healing. With a bit of knowledge, extra attention, and special care, my body took a positive turn. The physician trusted my levels and natural processes enough to release me. After the last labs were drawn, my body continued to recover. It so happens that my scar reveals the story of my healing.

I have another scar on my hip. The circumstances leading to this storyline were quite different. Racing in the school gym ended with my seven-year-old frame skidding across the floor. While I was old enough to remember the events leading to this scar, the experience required more than physical healing. My running and subsequent falling launched a trusted adult to annihilate me with words fueled by frustration. The scar on my hip was evidence of a physical wounding and healing, but it had implications the eye would never behold. Self-doubt, insecurity, and fear of making a mistake that would disappoint any adult from whom I desired approval, the invisible emotional scars, would continue to poke holes in my safety for decades.

Scars are storylines. Sometimes we get stuck licking the wound and miss the opportunity to experience healing, or we expend incredible amounts of energy hiding the scar. Sometimes the physical injury heals, but we cannot tell the story until the emotional wound heals. Maybe we are embarrassed about the part of our story that led to the scar, or it is simply too raw to share; some stories have to wait. There is no need to rush the process of healing.

Here is what I finally understand—there is enormous power in moments of solidarity that connect us to others. When I choose to share the story of a scar, literal or metaphorical, I open the door to vulnerability, and my struggles and victories become connection points. We tend to think we are the only ones with THAT struggle, but then we hear someone's scar storyline and suddenly consider the possibility of surviving the wounding.

Someone once told me that my fractured marriage scar gave them hope. Frankly, walking through a divorce and custody battle left me war-torn. I did not think I would ever heal, and even if healing came, I thought others would only see me as seriously injured for the rest of my life.

When we look at scars, we remember the wounding. When others see a scar, they see a story. Scars are the body's way of resolving a wound; they are a natural part of the healing process. While our scars tell of a time when something hard threatened our story, they are also evidence of our own healing process. The pain is the beginning of the story, not the end. Hard things do not have to take us out. Our storyline continues as we choose resilience and walk in the direction of healing. Tell someone your story; it invites continued healing within and provides hope without. You have no idea how much good can come from something that hurt deeply and healed completely.

One thing I have learned in my own journey of trauma healing is to avoid shortcuts around pain and insecurity. Dealing with disappointment and hurt requires consistent, hard work. Don't look the other way and hope for the best; out of sight, out of mind isn't the antidote for healing. Avoidance does not assure soul restoration. Avoidance happens to be inefficient. It prolongs the process of healing. When the shortcut looks far lovelier, stay the course.

Shortcuts offer the promise of a faster route and less work. As much as I love efficiency, some things in life require a long walk in the same direction. The decision to walk through the rough terrain is a long walk toward restoration. It may not be glamorous or efficient, but it is worth the effort.

What keeps us from pursuing healing? It is hard work, and without immediate results, we give up. We sacrifice using our voices to advocate for our own healing. Looking back over my life, I can identify multiple experiences when I did not use my voice.

● ● ●

Camp Widjiwagan was my home for one week, which was just enough time to sear the experience in my mind. Amid all the wonderful campfire songs, the sound of creaky cabin doors and floors, and glorious camp food, we also enjoyed daily pool time.

Since our cabins were far from the pool, we were transported by bus. In preparation for our afternoon trip to the pool, I rolled my clean clothes into a log with my undergarments discreetly tucked in the middle. Though an all-girl camp, no self-respecting eight-year-old wanted to expose her unmentionables to anyone.

After an hour or more of frolicking in the pool, the whistle called our attention to the lifeguard's announcement. It was time to exit the pool and get changed for dinner. The bus would take us from the pool to the mess hall, so an army of young girls filed into the tiny locker room to get changed. I grabbed my things and stood in line to wait for an open stall. After what felt like an eternity, one opened, and it was finally my turn.

I carefully unrolled my clothes to discover one item missing. Immediately, panic started rising at an accelerated rate. Paralyzed with fear, I did not know what to do, and I was not about to ask anyone standing in line to help me look for my underwear. To avoid humiliation, I decided to proceed without saying a word. I changed, boarded the bus, and hoped no one knew.

As the last girls boarded the bus, the camp director assumed her position at the front. What happened next is a moment I cannot erase. You know those moments that unfold in slow-motion? This was just like that. After counting girls, she held a single pair of underwear over her head and asked if anyone was missing them. My eyes darted around the bus. I was secretly praying someone would claim them. Anyone could have them; I wasn't picky. There was no way I was going to claim my property. I just wanted to melt into the seat until the moment passed.

While that was wildly embarrassing for my young self, something has always troubled me about that memory. What would keep me from claiming the property that was rightfully mine? No consequences were at stake for raising my hand. Seriously, it was not like she was holding up a pack of cigarettes that an eight-year-old should not have in the first place.

When I look back, I see a young girl who had lost her voice. A girl already consumed with the need to protect her image. I am still that girl in many respects. I do not want to look bad in front of others, so I sometimes take a step back when I should be stepping forward.

Do you know where image protection was rooted? The belief that I was bad and needed to keep others from finding out. That will silence a voice at any age. When you feel like you are a mistake, you do not feel worthy of speaking up, so fear tells you to shrink back to avoid feeling exposed.

Being voiceless and afraid is a heavy load to carry. I wish I could tell you I found my voice the following year, but I have spent over 40 years excavating the true me. Because I believed I was less than others, I carried myself that way. The girl who did not claim the underwear became the woman that would not advocate for the job she wanted. She mourned missed opportunities and dying dreams.

My "wasted years" required healing. Just as a broken bone must be set and cast, heart fractures require specific attention to maximize healing. Maybe you are limping through life with an old injury, and maybe you didn't even realize you lost your voice. It is not too late to reach for healing. It will require heavy lifting, but wholeness is possible.

You might not be in the position to claim those twice handed-down underwear, but you might be ready to reclaim your voice. Do not shrink back and let another day pass you by. Today is the perfect day to place your foot on the road to recovering the real you.

You can be someone different, choose something different, and live a different story. You must live your story, so you can tell the story. Be a living example of wisdom that emerged from weeds.

Relinquish your fear, tell your story, and be unleashed to be a beacon of hope in someone else's darkness.

REFLECTION: What is your story? Write a few lines of your story; avoid leaving out the hard part. If you can, share a portion of your story with a trusted person in your circle.

GOING DEEPER: Read John 4:1-42. What was the woman's story? How was it transformed? Where is the hope for a redeemed story found?

Chapter Fifteen

Dare to Take a Step

* Sometimes we need to put something
  down to let something else in.

*Faith is taking the first step even when you
don't see the whole staircase.*
—*Martin Luther King, Jr.*

MY HOME OFFICE IS SET UP at our kitchen table,
and I have the luxury of staring out at my backyard. I
live just outside the city, so I will call it the country for
the sake of this chapter. There are no houses behind
mine for five or more acres, so it is a quiet space. I
often watch the birds and deer with delight while
chasing off the persistent squirrels which cannot
accept that my bird feeders are not their cafeteria.

When I am not engrossed in my work, I pause and
stare quietly out the picture window. Before I even
realize it, I find myself dwelling on the deferred maintenance in my backyard. I feel the pull to cut down
dead branches, clean up the long-forgotten flower bed,
sweep the porch, fill the bird feeders, and lay sod in
the areas where grass once lived. Then I either change

my location or close the curtains because the need is overwhelming and outweighs my desire.

You have, no doubt, heard and repeated the phrase *out of sight, out of mind* many times. Its origin can be traced back to Homer, the Greek poet, if not further, so we have been wielding it a long time. The words imply that anything we do not see for an extended amount of time will be forgotten, but is that true? Maybe it is what we tell ourselves to feel better because there are things I haven't seen in a long time that crop up faster than unruly weeds after a spring shower.

- the backhanded compliment dripping from the lips of the trusted confidant
- the lapse of judgment resulting in a sexual encounter with an acquaintance
- the words released in anger that can't be taken back
- the shame of compromising a long-held conviction

All those thoughts are tied to another person or a group of people, and they creep in uninvited and overstay their welcome. That happens if you have seen the other party or not. Some of my most difficult memories are the hardest to put out of my mind—although nothing would be better than forgetting my failures and the painful offenses of others.

Out of sight, out of mind might be the biggest lie I have ever told myself, and yet there is something to the idea that what is in our vision has our attention. We tend to the things we can see. In that way, the *out of sight, out of mind* statement might be partially true. We are more likely to deal with things right in front of us. Just as I can obsess about the work that needs to be done in my backyard, I will put out all the small fires that present themselves daily without dealing with the spark that ignited the flame. The tangible wins my attention over the intangible.

Looking out my office window, I am also reminded that I create long lists of the work that needs to be done without ever taking a step to do it. I can complain about the unsightly mess all day long, but nothing changes if I never act on the need. If nothing changes, nothing changes. Closing the curtains and entertaining myself with videos of backyard makeovers, doesn't make the problem disappear. The need still exists. Just because we cannot see something doesn't mean it's not there. How often are we guilty of changing our view without tending to the need?

● ● ●

After my ex-husband moved out, I quickly removed most of the memories held in photographs. Except for a few in the children's rooms, I did not care for the reminder of what once was. We moved forward and began establishing a new identity as a family of three. It was the only thing I knew how to do, but it wasn't enough. Out of sight, out of mind didn't work for me because it didn't promote healing. Just when I thought I was turning a corner, a phone call or interaction with my ex took me back to square one. Not seeing the person who knew me most did not help me forget the pain of a broken relationship. I had to engage in the work of healing.

Like the deferred maintenance in my backyard, my wounded heart would not heal without my decision to step into it, get my hands dirty, and exert the effort to change the landscape of pain. *I could get bitter, or I could get better.* To get better, I had to admit my need, accept help through counseling, and dare to take a step of faith to believe healing was possible. Bitterness would grow from a heart not set on doing hard work or looking for a pathway out of the pain.

What keeps us from taking a step toward the work of healing? What keeps us from doing the next right thing? When I asked a group of women why they thought doing the work to move beyond the pain of their past was so difficult, the common response was rooted in a hesitancy to trust. It is dang hard to have the faith to believe the outcome will be worth the process. Most of us would gladly accept a healed heart, manicured lawn, or a clean slate, but we are resistant to the amount of work required to get through the process.

As a person who has done much work and with more to do, I am aware of a pattern of stopping short of the goal. I give up. Sometimes I stop before I have even started because I measure the payoff as not being worthy of the investment. Here's what I say to that version of any of us. Our healing is absolutely worth the investment. Taking the step and doing the work is about changing legacy. It is about living in abundance in the moment and not simply pining away for the time when things might change. Because here's the deal, our circumstances might not ever change.

For the view outside my window to change, I have to get involved. I have to invest in the process for the pain in my soul to subside. Things will slowly shift by taking one step at a time or making one decision at a time, but this requires belief and trust in the process and a sincere hope for the future. The opposite of out of sight, out of mind is a decision to observe the very thing we are avoiding. As it turns out, the very thing we are avoiding still impacts our journey.

● ● ●

On a road trip to visit our daughter and son-in-law, a lesson of this very kind emerged from an unexpected field trip into the weeds of life. We had greatly enjoyed our time with the kids, and we lingered longer than we should have before starting our first leg of the 1,000-mile trip home. As we pulled away from their apartment, we entered our destination into GPS and considered where to stop for dinner. I heard an unusual noise over our conversation, so I interrupted my husband and asked him what it was; he did not hear the noise that was so obvious to me. Because I could not let the concern go, I rolled down the window to get a better listen. By the sounds of the hissing and clicking with each tire rotation, something was stuck in one of our tires. We pulled over to take a look, and sure enough, there was a giant nut in our tire. It was 5:00 p.m. on Sunday, so panic set in as we realized the window of time for finding a garage was dwindling. We raced to Costco, and they made a concession to fix the tire even though it was past the time they took their last appointment.

We got on the road later than anticipated, and as we drove off, I had a thought percolating in my spirit. I had to roll my window down to allow the noise to come into the car. *Sometimes we need to put something down to let something else in.* How often had I missed growth opportunities because I wouldn't let go of the hurt or invite healing in? Putting something down is more than looking away from what is broken; it is looking at what is broken and deciding to take a step in a better direction.

When I put away the pictures after my divorce, there was a small hope that love would fill those frames again. Hope is a future assurance rooted in love. Proverbs 13:12 says, "hope deferred makes the heart sick." Without faith and hope, we probably won't take the necessary steps toward a redeemed past and better future, and we may settle into soul fatigue. Faith gives us the strength to take a step without seeing the path, and hope gives us the confidence to believe the next step will be laid out as we move forward.

What can you do today to encourage movement if you know you need to take a step? Some things you thought were out of sight, out of mind, are begging for your attention. Dare to take a step. You might stumble, but wisdom says to get up and try again. Take the chance. Healing is worth the investment. Hope will inflate as you dare to believe a better story is possible!

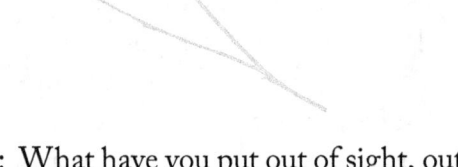

REFLECTION: What have you put out of sight, out of mind that needs your attention? Is there a step you feel prompted to take?

GOING DEEPER: Read Romans 5:3-5, Hebrews 10:23, and Proverbs 3:3-6. What is the source of your hope? What security do you have in taking a step and doing the work?

Acknowledgments

As you know, no book is birthed alone. There are many factors at work behind the scenes to bring a project to published form. I am grateful for those who have been a firm foundation under my feet for many years and those who have only just discovered that I write things. Here's to some of the greatest gifts in my life and along my path of healing and hope.

To every reader of my original "Moment of Truth Monday" posts and those who subscribe to my website or newsletter, thank you for sticking with me as I wrote my way out of the pit several years ago. Thank you for being my community. Your encouragement sustained my hope when I had little to draw from.

Members of the *Wisdom in the Weeds* launch team and those who read early copies of the manuscript, you have been such a gift to me during this process. You engaged with the content and provided feedback like it was your job. Thank you for your endorsements, presence, and steadfastness throughout the process.

Renee Johnsen, your feedback routinely landed in my inbox or DMs after reading a "Moment of Truth Monday" post. You encouraged me to write a book and offered to help. I absorbed your timely encouragement but kindly declined for a solid year or so. Then we began working on *Broken Vessels*, and your cheering took on a new form. You coached and challenged me to be a better writer and to communicate a clear story. Book number two would not have happened without you, Renee. What a gift you are to me.

Riki Yarbrough, I do not know anyone else who sees the world quite like you. Your creative genius is otherworldly, and I love that your fingerprints are all over this cover. Thank you for the time, expertise, and attention you gave this project. More than that, thank you for fanning my faith into flame through your faithful friendship.

Josie Barone, thank you for being a great friend and ministry partner. Your thoughtful questions and intentional encouragement have influenced me personally. *Broken Vessels* and the Sowkind Nonprofit have your fingerprints of love all over them. I am forever grateful for your sacrifices, cheering, and confidence.

Lisa Turner, not only were you my favorite boss, but you also taught me so much about leadership. If you had not trusted me to take over as the Writing Specialist on your campus, I would not have adequately nurtured my gift of writing. Thank you for believing in me then and now. I will always be grateful for the door you opened for me.

My former students made this book rich with meaning. Thank you to each of you who taught me more about wisdom than I could have learned by reading a book. Yes, I was your teacher, but I learned important life lessons as I observed how you viewed the world and engaged with others. We enjoyed community and connection in a way that is hard to duplicate in other settings, and I will hold your faces in my heart as long as I have breath.

Mentors are a large part of my healing story. They started pointing me toward Jesus when I was too stubborn to receive their guidance, and they continue to call me higher when I want to stoop low. Thank you, Joe and Ruthann Weece, for loving me through my middle years when trauma guided me more than kindness. Your investment is not lost on me. Denalyn Lucado, you took the baton during another hard season in my story. You mothered me and became the best "friendtor" I didn't even know I needed. Thank you for our four-hour dates and deep conversation. My life is richer because you are in it.

To my sisters, Vanessa Pohlman and Brigette Green, I love you more than words can say. Thank you for living the words in this book before they ever made it to print. You always show up. You always believe the best in me. You always make me better just by being in your presence. Thank you for holding space for me when we were young and afraid, and now when we don't have to be. Your lives influence mine in ways you may never fully know.

Nathan, Olivia, Maddy, Tip, and Andrew, what can truly be said about your love and influence in my life? As my children, you are a great source of joy. You teach me unique things about God every time you send a meme or chime in on our family group text. You bring the balance of fun to my overly serious side. Your lives point me back to the hope of the Gospel again and again. I will forever be the most obnoxious one in your cheering section. I love you.

John, you are more than my husband. You are a companion on this journey of healing. You get me like no one else quite does. You understand the look in my eyes that means I have drifted into a well-worn path, and you enter in. We have not always gotten it right, but I cherish the fact that we keep trying. We fail and succeed together, and there is no place I would rather be than together with you.

Thanks be to God for the gift of this life and the privilege of an eternal one. I boast only in your wisdom made available through surrender.

Scripture References

Chapter 1-John 14:27 NIV

Chapter 2-Philippians 4:1-8 NIV

Chapter 3-Psalm 23

Chapter 4-Luke 12:6-7, Isaiah 41:10

Chapter 5-Matthew 11:28-30, John 7:37-38

Chapter 6-Genesis 12:4, Proverbs 3:5-6

Chapter 7-John 3:16, Psalm 40:1-4

Chapter 8-Psalm 34

Chapter 9-Jeremiah 2:13, Romans 5:3-5

Chapter 10-Philippians 2:3, 1 Peter 4:8

Chapter 11-Isaiah 43:19

Chapter 12-Proverbs 16:24, Proverbs 12:25

Chapter 13-Luke 5:17-20

Chapter 14-John 4:1-42 NIV

Chapter 15-Proverbs 13:12, Romans 5:3-5,

Hebrews 10:23, and Proverbs 3:3-6

Endnotes

1. Shankar Vedantam, host *Hidden Brain* "How The 'Scarcity Mindset' Can Make Problems Worse," March 23, 2017, in *Morning Edition,* https://www.npr.org/2017/03/23/521195903/how-the-scarcity-mindset-can-make-problems-worse.

2. Brené Brown, *Daring Greatly: How the Courage to Be Vulnerable Transforms the Way We Live, Love, Parent, and Lead,* 1st ed. (New York: Gotham Books, 2012).

3. 1 Corinthians 10:23 NIV

4. Brené Brown, *The Gifts of Imperfection* (Minneapolis: Hazelden Information & Educational Services, 2010).

5. Steven Furtick "Certainty is knowing how. Confidence is knowing who," Facebook, March 8, 2021, https://www.facebook.com/StevenFurtick/posts/certainty-is-knowing-how-confidence-is-knowing-who-i-am-confident-of-this-philip/3973838495970869.

6 Dr. Anita Phillips, "Trauma" (Panel discussion, If:Gathering, Dallas, Texas, March 6, 2021).

7. Corrie Ten Boom, *The Hiding Place,* 35th Anniversary ed. (New York: Chosen Books, 2022), 31.

8. John Piper, "He is Like a Refiner's Fire," *Desiring God*, November 29, 1987, https://www.desiringgod.org/messages/he-is-like-a-refiners-fire.

9. Nicki Koziarz, *Flooded: The 5 Best Decisions to Make When Life Is Hard and Doubt Is Rising*, (Minneapolis: Bethany House, 2021).

10. Corrie ten Boom, "Guideposts Classics: Corrie ten Boom on Forgiveness," *Guideposts*, 1972, https://www.guideposts.org/better-living/positive-living/guideposts-classics-corrie-ten-boom-forgiveness.

About the Author

Alyssa De Los Santos is a writer, speaker, podcaster, and founder of the #Sowkind Movement. She is passionate about hope, truth, and restoration and loves encouraging others to lean into the fullness of who they were created to be. She believes every scar is a storyline that leads to connection and community, so she routinely shares her journey through broken seasons and the treasures she excavated along the way.

Alyssa lives in South Texas with her husband, youngest son, and one highly codependent furry friend. Her two oldest children are married and living actual adult lives in cities other than hers. She loves cheering for her people, eating chips and queso, drinking a good London Fog, and going on adventures in her vintage VW van.

Alyssa is a contributing author for *A Moment to Breathe: 365 Devotions That Meet You in Your Everyday Mess.* Her Bible study, *Broken Vessels: Reframing Brokenness to Advance the Gospel,* was released in 2021. You can find more of her work at www.alyssadelossantos.com.

alyssa_delossantos

AlyssaDeLosSantosTX

@alyssadelossantostx